Tenants' Rights

Tenants' Rights

A Guide for Washington State

Barbara A. Isenhour

James E. Fearn, Jr.

Steve Fredrickson

Illustrations by Charles D. Wood

UNIVERSITY OF WASHINGTON PRESS   Seattle and London

Library of Congress Cataloging in Publication Data
Isenhour, Barbara A   1947–
  Tenants' rights.

  Includes bibliographical references and index.
  1. Landlord and tenant—Washington (State)
2. Leases—Washington (State) I. Fearn, James E.,
1945–   joint author. II. Fredrickson, Steve,
1946–   joint author. III. Title.
KFW117.I84   346'.797'04342   77-73312
ISBN 0-295-95554-6

Acknowledgments

The authors wish to thank Linda Sutton of Evergreen Legal Services for her help in preparing this handbook for publication. We also express our appreciation to the National Housing Law Project (Berkeley, California), Myron Moskovitz, Ralph Warner, Charles E. Sherman, and the Nolo Press for permission to modify their form lease and rental agreement for use in Washington.

Contents

Tenants' Rights

Introduction

Is This Book for You?

This book is for Washington tenants—for anyone in this state who rents or leases a place to live. It is intended to help you understand your rights and responsibilities under Washington landlord-tenant law so that you will be able to deal more effectively with your landlord. We believe that unless tenants are well informed, they will not be able to take advantage of the rights and protections which the law provides. We also believe that when tenants understand their legal responsibilities, they can avoid many problems with their landlord.

While landlords will find this book useful, many of the rights and remedies provided landlords, as well as many of the problems they face, have not been fully discussed. One reason for this is that the professional landlord is more likely to have access to legal advice and information about his rights than the average tenant. We hope that this handbook will improve the odds a little.

What about Lawyers?

This book is not a substitute for lawyers. Although we have attempted to explain landlord-tenant law in plain, nonlegal language, it can be a complicated and confusing area of the law. We hope that this book will provide you with enough information and understanding so that you can intelligently decide whether or not you need to consult a lawyer.

If you need a lawyer but have little or no income, you may be eligible for legal aid or legal services representation. Legal Services offices in Washington are listed in Appendix C. Your county bar association can help you if you have trouble finding or selecting a lawyer.

Appendixes, Notes, and Glossary

A number of sample letters, notices, and court papers are included in this book. They are examples of documents that you may receive or be required to send. While some of the sample materials may be used as is, most of them must be adapted to fit your own circumstances. This is especially true of the sample legal documents.

In the back of the book you will find a model lease and a model month-to-month rental agreement. Before signing a written agreement prepared by your landlord, be sure to compare it with the model agreements, which are designed to be fair to both parties.

The Landlord-Tenant Act has been reproduced in full as Appendix A. Those who want to pursue any subject in more detail should look at the Act and also at the notes, where specific statutes, cases, and other reference materials are cited. For a brief definition of various legal terms you can consult the glossary.

1

Who Is Covered by
the Landlord-Tenant Act?

The rights and responsibilities of most tenants in residential housing are governed by the Residential Landlord-Tenant Act, which became law in 1973.[1] The Act was intended to modernize landlord-tenant law and to help ensure that adequate rental housing is available at a time when a growing number of people depend on rental housing for shelter. Before you rely on the information or advice in this handbook, you should determine whether you are covered by the Act.

A. Tenants Who Are Excluded from the Act

People who have the following living arrangements are not covered by the Landlord-Tenant Act:[2]

1. Renters of space in a mobile home park.[3] If you rent both the mobile home *and* the space from the same landlord, then you probably are covered by the Landlord-Tenant Act.
2. Residents in a dwelling under an earnest money agreement, option to purchase,[4] or contract to buy the property.
3. Residents in a medical, religious, educational, recreational, or correctional institution.
4. Residents in a hotel, motel, or boarding house.
5. Migrant workers whose housing is provided by their employer.
6. Tenants who are employed on the premises by their landlord and are allowed to live there only because of the job (an example would be a live-in maid).

5

7. Tenants who rent housing but are primarily renting the land for farming.
8. Tenants who rent property for commercial purposes rather than residential purposes.
9. Tenants who are leasing a single family dwelling for a year or more, provided that their exemption from the Act has been approved by their attorney.[5]

B. Does It Make Any Difference if You Aren't Covered by the Act?

Tenants who are covered by the Landlord-Tenant Act have many rights and remedies that are not available to tenants who are excluded from the Act. Particularly if you are faced with an eviction action, it can make a substantial difference whether or not you are covered by the Act. If you are not covered by the Act and rent is found to be owing in an eviction action, the judge can make you pay double the amount of rent owing.[6] Doubling the amount of rent owing is prohibited under the Landlord-Tenant Act.[7] Also, your landlord may be able to get a court order for the sheriff to evict you without first giving you a chance to tell your story to a judge.[8] Under the Landlord-Tenant Act, a hearing is required before a judge will sign an order for the sheriff to evict you.[9]

If your landlord sues you and wins, the amount of attorney's fees you may have to pay will vary substantially depending on whether or not you are covered by the Landlord-Tenant Act. If you are not covered by the Act you will only have to pay a nominal fee to your landlord's attorney (unless you have a lease or rental agreement which provides that you will pay your landlord's "reasonable attorney's fee" if you lose). This nominal attorney's fee is $35 in superior court and $25 in district court.[10] Under the Landlord-Tenant Act, if you lose certain lawsuits you may have to pay your landlord's "reasonable attorney's fees."[11] These fees will depend on how many hours the attorney spent on the case but it is not uncommon for attorneys to charge $35 to $50 per hour for their services. Preparation for a trial and the trial itself might easily take ten hours, and in complicated cases even longer. Thus your landlord's "reasonable attorney's fees" could be $500 or more.

Certain issues discussed in this handbook are applicable to *all* tenants regardless of whether they are covered by the Landlord-Tenant Act. The issues include:

1. Retaliatory actions by landlords.
2. Warranty of habitability.
3. Discrimination by landlords.
4. Locking tenants out or taking their property.
5. Landlord's liability if a tenant is injured or his property is damaged because of the landlord's negligence.

2

Moving In

A. Making the Initial Inspection

Before entering into an agreement with a landlord, you should carefully inspect the place. Remember that serious problems are not always obvious. Potential problems that sometimes go unnoticed include the following:

1. Inadequate water pressure.
2. Inadequate hot water.
3. Leaks in the plumbing.
4. Locks that do not function properly.
5. Light fixtures and wall sockets that do not work.
6. Too few garbage cans.
7. Leaking basements and roofs.
8. Insect or rodent infestation.

You should speak to the tenants who are moving out of the place and to other tenants in the building to see if they have had problems with the unit, the building, other tenants, or the landlord. If you suspect serious problems with the building you can check with your local building department and see if they have any record of housing code violations for that building. In Seattle, the building department maintains files by address. The files are available to the public for inspection.

If you spot a problem during the initial inspection, ask your landlord if he plans to repair it and when the repair will be completed. If your landlord promises to make the repair, it may be wise to get him to put the promise in writing and sign it. You might also ask your landlord to agree to a rent reduction or other type of compensation in case the repair is not made.

EXAMPLE: I, Mr. Smith, agree to repair the broken window in apartment 3 by September 1st and if I don't, Mary Jones may deduct $5.00 per day from her rent for each day that I fail to replace the window after that date.

B. Reaching an Agreement with Your Landlord

Before you move in, you should try to reach an understanding with the landlord on the rules and regulations which you will be required to follow. There is no point in moving in if the landlord has a rule which you know you will not be able to obey. While you can try to negotiate with the landlord about rules and regulations, keep in mind that tenants are usually in a weak bargaining position. The landlord may decide not to rent to you at all if he feels your requests are unacceptable to him.

Here is a list of things that should be discussed *before* you agree to move in:

1. How much is the rent and when is it to be paid?
2. Are there any late charges for delinquent rent?
3. Is there a deposit, if so how much, and how and when will it be refunded?
4. Who will pay for what utilities (water, heat, electricity, gas, garbage collection, sewer, telephone)?
5. Is the tenancy for a fixed period (like one year) or is it for an indefinite period?
6. What are the rules on pets, guests, parking, etc.?
7. What repairs or cleaning does your landlord agree to complete before you move in?

C. Types of Tenancies

The two most common types of residential tenancies are month-to-month tenancies and tenancies for a fixed period.[1] The agreement you reach with your landlord will determine the type of tenancy you have. It is important for you and your landlord to have a clear understanding about the type of tenancy you have because that will determine what your rights and duties are under the Landlord-Tenant Act and other laws.

1. Month-to-Month Tenancy

If you have agreed to pay rent on a monthly basis and have not agreed to stay for a specific period of time, then you have a month-to-month tenancy.[2] This agreement can be either oral or written. Either you or your landlord may end the tenancy at any time by giving the other written notice at least twenty days before the end of the rental period. Your landlord may increase the rent or change the rules at any time as long as he first gives you written notice at least thirty days before the end of the rental period which precedes the effective date of the rule change or rent increase. The procedure for increasing the rent or changing the rules is discussed in more detail on pages 20 and 22.

2. Tenancy for a Fixed Period

If you have an agreement with your landlord to stay for a *fixed* period of time, then you have what is called a tenancy for a specific period.[3] This type of agreement is commonly called a *lease*. To be valid, a lease must be in writing. An oral agreement for a specific term is not a valid lease and creates only a month-to-month tenancy.[4] If the agreement is to be in effect for more than one year, then it must not only be in writing but must also be signed by the landlord before a notary public. During the fixed period of time, rent cannot be increased and the rules of the tenancy cannot be changed unless *both* you and your landlord agree.

As a tenant for a fixed period, you have made a promise to your landlord that you will not move out before the period expires. In return, your landlord has promised not to evict you before the end of the term as long as you do not violate any provisions in the lease.

D. Month-to-Month Tenancy versus Tenancy for a Fixed Period

If you are in a weak bargaining position, you may not be able to choose whether you will be a month-to-month tenant or a tenant for a fixed term. It is still helpful to be aware of the advantages and disadvantages of each type of tenancy. The type of tenancy that is best for you will depend in part on what your primary concerns are.

If you are concerned about being able to stay in one place for a specific period of time or if you are concerned about the possibility of your rent being raised every few months, a lease may be the best type of agreement for you. There is a price to pay for this security. If you change your mind after moving in and decide that you want to move out, you may be responsible to your landlord for additional rent. (This is discussed in more detail in chapter 8.) If you want the freedom to move on twenly days notice, then a month-to-month tenancy may be the best arrangement for you. Some problems with a month-to-month tenancy are that your landlord can ask you to move, increase your rent, or change the rules at any time as long as the proper advance notice is given.

E. Written Leases or Rental Agreements

Your landlord may ask you to sign a document when you move in. A written agreement helps to avoid later disputes about the rules and conditions of the tenancy. If you are a month-to-month tenant this document is called a rental agreement.[5] If you are a tenant for a fixed period this document is usually called a lease. Some landlords confuse leases with rental agreements or use the terms interchangeably so you should not rely on the way the document is labeled. Whether you are a month-to-month tenant or a tenant for a fixed period will depend on the terms of the document rather than what it is called.

Read the written agreement carefully!

If there is something in the lease or rental agreement that you disagree with, *do not sign it.* Once you sign a lease or rental agreement you will ordinarily be bound by its terms except for provisions which are illegal under the Landlord-Tenant Act.[6] If your landlord tells you not to worry about a clause that you consider unacceptable, you should ask that it be crossed out on all copies of the agreement and have your landlord initial the lined-out parts. Also, if your landlord makes additional promises not included in the written agreement, these promises may not be legally enforceable unless they are added to the written document. Once you sign an agreement, it is assumed that the document includes *all* agreements made up to the time you sign the paper, and you ordinarily cannot later claim that there were other agreements made at the same time that modify, vary, or contradict what is in the written document.[7] We have included a model lease and rental agreement in this

handbook as Appendix D. Before signing a written agreement prepared by your landlord, you should compare it with the model agreements, which are designed to be fair to both parties. Ask about any requirements in your landlord's form that do not appear in the model agreements. Better yet, see if you can persuade the landlord to use one of the model agreements instead of his.

F. Rental Agreements That Look like a Lease

Some month-to-month tenants have rental agreements with a clause that states that if the tenant does not stay for a minimum number of months (usually six), he forfeits the deposit. Be aware that this clause does not mean that your rental agreement is a lease. Many tenants who have this type of rental agreement are shocked to find out that their landlord can give them a twenty-day eviction notice or change the rent or rules during the six-month period.

While you may have promised to stay for six months or forfeit your deposit, your landlord has made no similar promise that you will be *allowed* to stay for six months. If the agreement were a lease, both you and your landlord would have made a promise that the term of the tenancy was at least six months, and that the rent and rules would remain the same for that time.

G. Illegal Provisions to Watch Out for in Your Lease or Rental Agreement

The Landlord-Tenant Act expressly prohibits the following clauses in a rental agreement or lease:[8]

1. An agreement to waive your rights under the Landlord-Tenant Act.
2. An agreement that if your landlord files a lawsuit against you, you will not contest it.
3. An agreement to pay your landlord's attorney's fees in situations not authorized by the Landlord-Tenant Act.
4. An agreement to limit the landlord's responsibility in case of injury, accident, or damage, where the landlord is liable. (This is called an "exculpatory clause.")
5. An agreement to accept a particular arbitrator if you and your landlord should later decide to resolve a dispute through arbitration.

If your lease or rental agreement has any of the five clauses mentioned above, your landlord cannot enforce them. If you are damaged as a result of relying on an illegal clause, you can sue to recover your financial losses as well as reasonable attorney's fees.[9] Some clauses that appear in a lease or rental agreement are not expressly prohibited by the Landlord-Tenant Act but are still unenforceable. Some unenforceable clauses that often appear in form leases and rental agreements include the following:

1. An agreement that your landlord can take your property if you get behind in your rent.
2. An agreement allowing your landlord to come into your place at any time, without notice.
3. An agreement that you will pay for all damage to your place, regardless of whether it was your fault.
4. An agreement that if your landlord has to take you to court, you will pay double the amount the court decides you owe.

You and your landlord can agree that certain sections of the Landlord-Tenant Act will not apply to your tenancy.[10] These sections are:

1. Duties of the landlord;
2. Duties of the tenant;
3. Repair remedies for the tenant; and
4. Notice to a tenant who is not performing his duties as a tenant.

If you don't want one of these sections to apply to your tenancy you must first follow a specific procedure set out in the Landlord-Tenant Act. Keep in mind that no rights or duties under the Act can be waived in a *form* lease or rental agreement.[11]

3

Landlord Duties

A. What Does the Landlord-Tenant Act Require?

The Landlord-Tenant Act requires your landlord to provide you with a decent, safe, and reasonably clean place to live.[1] He cannot avoid these requirements by shifting the responsibility to you or anyone else.[2] The Act says that your landlord has to keep your place fit for human habitation and in particular he must:

1. Correct violations of any health code and housing code standards and any other laws and regulations which endanger the tenants' health or safety.
2. Make sure the place is structurally sound and the roof, floor, walls, chimneys, fireplaces, and foundations are in good repair.
3. Keep the common areas like apartment hallways, laundry rooms, and parking lots reasonably clean, sanitary, and safe from defects that could cause fires or other accidents.
4. Make sure the place is not infested by rodents, insects, and other pests when the tenant moves in, and, except in the case of a single family residence, control infestation during the tenancy.
5. Keep the place in as good repair as it was or should have been when you moved in, except for normal wear and tear.
6. Provide adequate locks and keys.
7. Keep the electrical, plumbing, and heating systems in good repair and repair any appliances or other facilities that are supplied.
8. Keep the place reasonably weathertight.
9. Provide garbage cans and arrange for trash removal for everyone other than tenants who occupy single family residences.

15

10. Provide facilities that are adequate to supply a reasonable amount of heat, water, and hot water, unless the building is not equipped to supply these utilities.

Your landlord also has a duty to tell you his name and address either by a statement on the rental agreement or by a notice posted in some conspicuous place on the premises.

B. What Does Local Law Require?

You should check to see if there are any local laws or regulations in your area which impose additional duties on landlords or duties that are more specific than the ones in the Landlord-Tenant Act. If a local code, ordinance, or regulation imposes a stricter standard on landlords than the Landlord-Tenant Act, the landlord must abide by the stricter standard. The Seattle Housing Code is an example of a local code that imposes more specific duties on landlords than the Landlord-Tenant Act.[3] It states, for instance, that where heating is supplied by the owner, a temperature of at least 65 degrees Fahrenheit must be maintained in Seattle housing units from 7:00 a.m. to 10:30 p.m. during the period from September 1 to June 30. In addition, it contains specific requirements for light and ventilation, plumbing, electrical equipment, entrance and exit doors, and door locks—requirements intended to make rental housing safer and more secure.

C. When Must Your Landlord Make Repairs?

Your landlord does *not* have a duty to repair defects which were caused by you or your family or guests.[4] He also has no duty to make repairs if you unreasonably refuse to let him enter your place to correct the problems. As a general rule, if something needs to be repaired in or around your place, it is your landlord who is responsible for repairing it. The exceptions are if the problem is caused by normal wear and tear or by your own intentional or careless behavior.

Repair problems often occur with stoves, refrigerators, or other appliances. Even though there is no law that requires landlords to provide tenants with a stove, refrigerator, or any other appliance, once the landlord provides the appliance he has a duty to repair it if something goes wrong with it. The landlord can't escape this duty by trying to shift the repair responsibility to the tenant or by providing the appliance only on an "as is" basis. But if your landlord can show that the appliance broke down because you used it improperly then you could be required to pay for the repairs. Your landlord also has a duty to take care of problems with the plumbing, heating, or electrical systems unless he can show that you caused the problem.

Some problems that come up are not the fault of either you or your landlord. In those situations it is usually the landlord who is going to have to take care of the problem and pay for the repairs.

> EXAMPLE: Someone has thrown a rock through your living-room window. It is not normal wear and tear so unless your landlord can show that you or someone under your control broke the window, he is going to have to pay to replace it.

In this example it is not your landlord's fault that the window was broken but it is his responsibility to repair it because he must keep the place weathertight and in good repair.

4

Tenant Duties

A. Your Duty to Take Care of Your Place

As a tenant, you have certain duties under the Landlord-Tenant Act.[1] You must:

1. Comply with obligations that are imposed on tenants by any city, county, or state laws or regulations.[2]
2. Keep the place you occupy clean and sanitary.
3. Regularly remove garbage and rubbish from the place.
4. Pay for extermination or fumigation if your place is infested and it is your fault.
5. Properly use and operate the plumbing, electrical, and heating systems, and the appliances and fixtures supplied by your landlord.
6. Not intentionally or carelessly damage the place or let anyone else damage it.
7. Not permit a nuisance or waste.[3]
8. When you move out, put the place back in its original condition except for normal wear and tear.
9. Obey all reasonable rules and regulations that are called to your attention when you move in or are later adopted by your landlord.

B. What if You Don't Perform These Duties?

If you don't perform these duties, your landlord can take certain actions against you.[4] He may:

1. Sue you for damages.
2. Submit a dispute over duties to arbitration, if you agree to arbitrate.

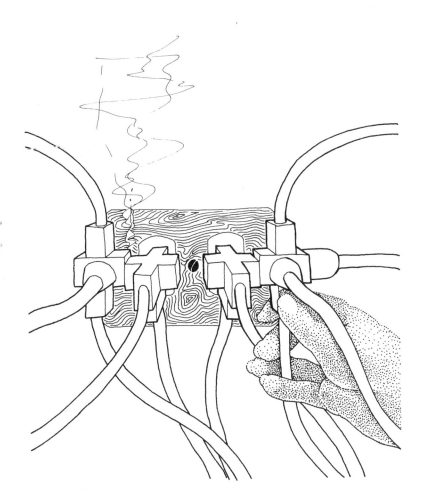

3. Evict you after giving you proper notice.

In addition, if you have a duty to correct a problem and it is a problem that can be remedied by repair, replacement of a damaged item, or cleaning, your landlord may be able to correct the problem himself and add the cost to your rent.[5] Your landlord can only take this action if your failure to correct the problem could substantially affect your health and safety or the health and safety of other tenants or substantially increase the hazards of fire or accident. Your landlord has to follow certain procedures to use this remedy. He must:

1. Give you a written notice describing the duties you have failed to perform.
2. Wait thirty days to give you a chance to correct the problem yourself. (You can be required to correct the problem sooner if it is an emergency.)

If you have not corrected the problem after your landlord has given you written notice and waited the proper period of time, he can enter your place, have the work done, and submit an itemized bill to be payable along with your next month's rent. You and he can also negotiate terms for payment, but if your rental agreement has terminated, the bill is payable immediately.

C. Paying Your Rent

One of your duties as a tenant is to pay your rent on time. The law doesn't say when you have to pay it so it is up to you and the landlord to agree on the time. The general rule is that unless there is an agreement to the contrary, rent is due at the end of the term, although most landlords require that you pay rent in advance at the beginning of each month.[6] If you don't pay on time your landlord can serve you with a three-day notice to pay rent or vacate, and start an eviction action. Sometimes landlords are willing to accept rent late, especially if you have a good excuse, but landlords are legally entitled to ask for prompt payment no matter how good your excuse. A court can order you to be evicted even if it was not your fault that you couldn't pay.

1. Late Charges

If you don't pay your rent on time, your landlord may require you to pay a "late charge." Your landlord can't force you to pay a late charge unless you have signed a lease or rental agreement which allows the charge or unless the late charge was called to your attention when you moved in. The Landlord-Tenant Act doesn't put any limit on the amount of late charges but they must be reasonable.[7] The arguments against deposits which amount to penalties can also be made about unreasonable late charges (see page 52).

2. Rent Increases

Some states and cities have rent control laws limiting the

amount of rent a landlord can charge and restricting the circumstances under which rent can be increased. There are no such laws in Washington right now. However, if you live in public housing or certain types of government subsidized housing you may only be required to pay a maximum of 25 percent of your income for rent.[8] If you and your landlord have agreed on a rent amount and you have a lease for a fixed period like six months or one year, then your landlord can't increase the rent until the end of the period. If you are a month-to-month tenant, there is no restriction on how much or how often your landlord can increase the rent, as long as proper notice is given, unless you can show the increase is retaliatory or discriminatory.[9]

If you are a month-to-month tenant, your landlord has to give you written notice of a rent increase at least thirty days before the end of the rental period.[10]

EXAMPLE: You are a month-to-month tenant and your rental period is from the first of the month through the last day of the month. If your landlord wants to raise your rent on October 1, he must give you thirty days written notice before the end of September. This means he would have to give you notice on or before August 31.

The notice period begins on the day *following* the day on which the notice is served.[11] If your landlord gives you less than thirty days notice of a proposed rent increase, the rent increase is not effective and the landlord cannot legally evict you for refusing to pay the increased amount. However, the notice of the increase could be valid for the following month. In the example cited above, if the landlord gave you written notice of a rent increase on September 15, he could not legally increase the rent on October 1, but he probably could increase the rent on November 1 without further notice.

Sometimes a landlord will give month-to-month tenants a twenty-day notice that he is terminating their tenancy along with an offer to let them stay if they agree to pay a higher rent or agree to a change in rules and regulations. This type of notice is used as a way of getting around the requirement of giving thirty days notice of a proposed rule change or rent increase. There is nothing in the Landlord-Tenant Act that specifically makes this procedure illegal, although deliberate avoidance of the thirty-day notice requirement violates the spirit of the Act.[12]

If you decide to move out rather than pay the increased rent, you are still required to give your landlord written notice that you are moving, at least twenty days before the end of your rental period. Notices to terminate a tenancy are discussed in more detail on page 44.

D. Rules and Regulations

1. Your Duty to Obey the Rules

You are required to obey all reasonable rules and regulations which your landlord sets up. The rules can't be in violation of the Landlord-Tenant Act or some other law and must be called to your attention when you move in.[13] They don't have to be in writing and they don't have to be posted.

It is hard to give any useful guidelines to help you decide what kind of rule is unreasonable. In general, if a rule is designed to protect the privacy or comfort of other tenants or to make sure you properly maintain your place, it is probably going to be considered reasonable. There is no law which requires landlords to rent to people with children. Rules which prohibit tenants from having pets are also legal.[14] Landlords may also have rules which tell you when to stop playing your radio or stereo or which prohibit you from hanging pictures or mirrors without first getting permission. A rule is not enforceable if it is prohibited by the Act or if it discriminates against tenants on the basis of race, creed, color, national origin, sex, marital status, or the presence of any sensory, mental, or physical handicap.[15]

2. How Your Landlord Changes the Rules

If you are a month-to-month tenant, your landlord can adopt a new rule or change an old rule by giving you a written notice at least thirty days before the end of your rental period.

> EXAMPLE: You are a month-to-month tenant and pay your rent on the first of every month. Your landlord has adopted a new rule that as of June 1 no pets will be allowed in the building. Your landlord must give you written notice of this rule change on or before May 1.

The rule change can't be retaliatory.[16] Keep in mind that if you have a lease, rules can only be changed during the term of the lease by agreement between you and your landlord.

If you decide to move out rather than obey the new rule, you are still required to give your landlord written notice that you are moving, at least twenty days before the end of your rental period. Notices to terminate a tenancy are discussed in more detail on page 44.

5

What to Do
about Repair Problems

A. Introduction

Although many landlords are interested in maintaining their buildings and are willing to make necessary repairs promptly, you should know your rights when dealing with a reluctant landlord. Hopefully, you will be able to get repairs made with just a telephone call or conversation with your landlord. Not all landlords expect or insist on formal written notices requesting repairs. Before you can take any action against an uncooperative landlord, however, a *written* notice to repair is usually required. There may also be a fairly long waiting period after the written notice is given before you can take any action. The length of the notice period depends on the seriousness of the problem. The sooner you give written notice the better.

You have a number of alternatives if your landlord fails or refuses to make required repairs. The alternatives include:

1. Deducting repair costs from your rent;
2. Suing your landlord;
3. Getting your landlord to agree to arbitration;
4. Reporting your landlord to the local building department or health department;
5. Moving out;
6. Withholding rent.

The procedures for each approach are described below. You should decide which remedy is most practical after considering all the alternatives. Your landlord may not be happy about your use of any of these remedies and you should be aware of the possibility of retaliation or reprisal.

B. Self-help Repair

If the defect that needs to be repaired is something that you can handle without any help and is not too expensive to fix, you may be able to make the repairs yourself and deduct the cost from your next month's rent. You can only use this remedy if you are current in your rent and utilities.[1] To do this you have to take the following steps.

1. Written Notice to Repair

You must deliver to your landlord a written notice to repair which contains the following information:[2]

1. Your address and apartment number.
2. The name of the owner, if known.
3. A description of the problem.

You should sign the notice and keep a copy for yourself.

2. Delivering the Notice

Your landlord's name and address are supposed to be on your rental agreement or conspicuously posted where you live.[3] The notice to repair can be delivered either to the landlord or to the person who collects your rent. The law doesn't say how the notice must be delivered. It can be mailed or delivered personally. It is best to hand it to your landlord. That way you know he actually received the notice and you know the date on which it was received.

3. Waiting Period

How much time your landlord is allowed before he must start making repairs depends on the seriousness of the problem. Except when there are circumstances beyond his control,[4] your landlord must start repairs within the following time periods:

1. *Twenty-four hours* when you are deprived of water or heat or when the problem is extremely hazardous to life (for example gas leaking from your furnace).

July 21, 1977

TO: J. Landlord
      1434 Park Place
      Seattle, WA 98104

      Please take notice that the dwelling unit which
you own and which I occupy located at 718 Baltic Street,
Apt. H, Seattle, Washington 98144, contains the following defects:

              1. Broken toilet;

              2. Broken kitchen window;

              3. Leaky bedroom radiator;

              4. Crumbling plaster on living-
                  room ceiling;

              5. Defective left rear stove burner.

      If these problems are not corrected within a
reasonable period of time, I intend to use the remedies
provided in the Landlord-Tenant Act.

                        Sincerely,

                        B. Tenant

Notice to repair

2. *Forty-eight hours* when there is no hot water or electricity.
3. *Seven days* when the repair can be made for $75 or one-half of one month's rent, whichever is less, assuming your landlord is not required to repair the problem sooner under (1) or (2).
4. *Thirty days* in all other cases.

Once your landlord starts the repairs, the work must be completed within a reasonable period of time.

4. Performing the Work

If you have delivered a written notice, waited the required time period as described above, and have still gotten no results, you can make the repairs yourself and deduct the cost from the rent.[5] This remedy can be used when:

1. The cost of repair including labor[6] and materials does not exceed the lesser of one-half of one month's rent or $75; and
2. The law does not require that the repair be performed by a licensed or registered person; and
3. The problem to be repaired is within the leased premises; and
4. You are current in your rent and utilities.

After you have completed the repairs in a workmanlike manner and have given your landlord an opportunity to inspect, you can deduct the cost of the repairs from the rent. Be careful about trying to make difficult repairs on your own. The work performed must meet the requirements imposed by applicable codes, statutes, ordinances, or regulations. Your landlord can hold you responsible if the repairs were not performed properly.

5. Limit on Repairs

Under the self-help repair and deduct procedure, the maximum amount that you can deduct from rent during any twelve-month period is $75 or one-half of one month's rent, whichever is less.

> EXAMPLE: If your rent is $200 per month the maximum dollar amount of deductible repairs which you can make yourself during a twelve-month period would be $75. You could make one repair at a cost of $75 or five separate repairs at a cost of $15 each. If your rent is $100 per month the maximum deduction for a year under this section would be $50.

C. Hiring Someone to Make Repairs

If you are unable or unwilling to make repairs yourself, you can hire someone to make the repairs and then deduct the cost from your rent.[7] You must be current in rent and utilities to use this remedy. The procedure for hiring someone to make repairs is similar to the procedure for self-help repairs. You must deliver a written notice and wait the required period of time as described on pages 26 and 28 before taking further action. In addition, you have to submit bids for the repair work.

1. Getting Bids

The law requires that you obtain at least two bids for the repair work. Each bid must be from a person who is licensed or registered to make the kinds of repairs you need. If the type of work you want done does not require a licensed or registered repairperson, then any capable person can make the repairs. An example of a repair that requires a licensed repairperson would be rewiring.

2. Delivering the Bids

The law requires that bids either be delivered to the landlord or his designated agent personally or be sent by certified mail. They may be submitted to the landlord with the notice to repair.

3. Waiting Period

If your landlord has not started making repairs within the required period of time and if you have sent the required bids, you may have the repairs performed by the person submitting the lowest bid. When your landlord has thirty days to start repairs you cannot have those repairs done until thirty days after your landlord receives your notice to repair or fifteen days after he receives your bids, whichever is later.

> EXAMPLE: If your landlord has thirty days to start making repairs and you deliver the notice to repair *and* the required bids on January 1, you could have repairs started on February 1. If the notice to repair is delivered on January 1 and the bids are not delivered until January 16, you could still start the repairs on February 1. If the notice to repair is delivered on January 1 and the bids are not delivered until January 31, then you could not start the repairs until February 16.

4. Performing the Work

After the person you hire completes the repairs, your landlord must be given an opportunity to inspect the work. Once your landlord has had an opportunity to inspect, you can deduct the cost of the repairs from the rent.

5. Limit on Repairs

The total rent deduction allowed under the bid repair remedy cannot be more than one month's rent during any twelve month period. The bid repair remedy cannot be used when your landlord fails to provide adequate locks and keys or appropriate trash receptacles.

D. Combining Repair Remedies

The maximum amount you can deduct from your rent under the self-help repair remedy or bid repair remedy is not very much. If you have several problems, you can use both remedies and deduct the maximum amount under each one.[8] If you live in an apartment building where there are problems which affect many tenants, like a broken furnace or dilapidated common areas, a number of tenants may join together and send notices to repair and bids to the landlord and combine their rent deductions so more expensive repairs can be made.

> EXAMPLE: If the tenants in a building pay $100 a month in rent and it would cost $300 to repair a furnace that fails to provide adequate heat to the entire building, one tenant could only make a maximum rent deduction of $100 under the bid repair remedy. But if ten tenants who are affected by the lack of heat join in a notice to repair and submit bids, they could each deduct $30 from their rent and the repair could be made.

E. Suing Your Landlord

1. Claims under the Landlord-Tenant Act

If requested repairs have not been made, you can file a lawsuit against your landlord.[9] You must be current in rent and utilities, have delivered a notice to repair, and have waited the required time period, as described on pages 26 and 28. The court may be able to help you in one of the following ways:[10]

1. It can find that the rental value of your place has been reduced as a result of repair problems and order your landlord to refund any excess rent you have paid since delivery of your notice to repair.
2. It can order your landlord to pay for repairs you have made under the self-help repair or bid repair procedure if you have not already deducted those costs from your rent.
3. It can authorize you to make repairs or have repairs made and deduct the costs from your rent up to a maximum of one month's rent in any calendar year.
4. It can reduce your rent until your landlord makes necessary repairs.

The court also has the power to decide that repair problems are so bad that your landlord cannot, as a practical matter, correct them within a reasonable period of time. If the court determines that you should not remain in your place in its defective condition it can authorize termination of your tenancy and require you to move out within a reasonable time.

You can bring a lawsuit against your landlord in either district court or superior court. If the claim is for the recovery of money and the amount you are asking for is $300 or less, you can sue in small claims court.

2. The Implied Warranty of Habitability

The Washington Supreme Court has ruled that even though a landlord does not expressly agree to make repairs, he has an obligation to provide a livable place.[11] This obligation is called an "implied warranty of habitability" and operates independently of the Landlord-Tenant Act. It applies to all rental housing and cannot be bargained away by a tenant even in exchange for a lower rent.

There is no specific standard for determining when the "implied warranty of habitability" has been violated. If a problem or combination of problems makes your place dangerous or threatens your health or safety and you decide to sue your landlord, the court could rule that your place is partially or totally uninhabitable. Minor inconveniences or problems which only affect the appearance of your place will normally not support a claim of uninhabitability.

To the extent your landlord provides a dwelling unit that is totally or partially uninhabitable as a result of unrepaired defects, you are relieved of the obligation to pay all or part of the agreed rent. If you have paid more rent than should have been required, you can sue to recover the excess.[12] It is hard to accurately determine what portion of the rent you should get back. If you file a lawsuit to recover excess rent, a judge will generally arrive at a refund figure based on the seriousness of the defects, the amount of inconvenience you were caused, and the length of time the defects existed. Before filing a lawsuit, you should try to determine how much the rental value of your place was reduced as a result of the condition making it wholly or partially uninhabitable.

> EXAMPLE: You rented a place at an agreed rent of $100 per month. After moving in you discovered a number of defects including a leaky toilet, leaky roof, inoperable stove, and lack of heat in one bedroom. You notified your landlord about the problems but no repairs were made. You continued to pay the agreed rent of $100 per month for four months. Finally, you got fed up and determined that the premises had a reduced rental value of only $75 per month over the last four months. Assuming that a $25 rent reduction was reasonable, you could sue to recover the excess rent paid over the four month period, which would be $25 per month for a total of $100.

It is not necessary for you to submit a notice to repair or be current in rent if your lawsuit is based on violation of the "implied warranty of habitability." Those requirements only apply when you are using a remedy contained in the Landlord-Tenant Act.[13] Nevertheless, it is generally a good idea to follow the written notice to repair procedures if you have the opportunity to do so.

F. Submitting Repair Disputes to Arbitration

You and your landlord can agree to have a repair dispute decided by an arbitrator rather than a judge.[14] The arbitration agreement must be in writing and the person chosen to act as arbitrator must be selected after the dispute occurs. Any written or oral agreement naming a particular person to arbitrate future disputes is not binding on either you or your landlord.[15] You cannot use the arbitration procedure unless you are current in your rent and utilities. A notice to repair must be delivered to your landlord and you must wait the period of time required by the Act as described on pages 26 and 28 before arbitration can begin.

Arbitrators of repair disputes have practically the same powers as judges. They can authorize you to make repairs which cost more than those allowed by the Act, reduce your rent until repairs are made, or order your landlord to refund a portion of the rent you have paid if they find that you have paid more rent than your place was worth.

The arbitration procedure is complicated. Certain types of repair disputes cannot be decided by arbitration. Because arbitration is seldom used and is difficult to explain simply, it will not be discussed in detail in this book. If you are interested in using the arbitration procedure you should consult the Landlord-Tenant Act and the law on arbitration in general.[16]

G. Reporting Your Landlord to Local Agencies

If your landlord fails to make necessary repairs or provide necessary services, it is possible that the failure violates city or county building codes, housing codes, or health codes. The agencies which administer those codes may be able to use their enforcement powers to get defects corrected or impose penalties for failure to make necessary repairs. You should contact the appropriate agencies in your area and submit a written request for an inspection. The request should include the address of the property you want inspected, a description of the problems, and your own name, address, and telephone number. Those agencies may be able to get your landlord to make necessary repairs.

H. Moving Out

If your landlord fails to make necessary repairs you can also move out. If you are current in rent and utilities, have given a notice to repair and waited the required period of time, as described on pages 26 and 28, and no repairs have been started by your landlord, you can give your landlord written notice and move out of your place immediately.[17] The notice can either be mailed or delivered personally. This remedy can be used regardless of whether you have a month-to-month rental agreement or a lease for a specific term. It doesn't make any difference whether the rental agreement is oral or written. Once you give written notice and move out you have no obligation to pay any more rent. In addition, you are entitled to a *pro rata* refund of any rent which

July 22, 1977

Department of Buildings
Room 408
Seattle Municipal Building
Seattle, Washington 98104

Dear Inspector:

It is urgent that you inspect my apartment located
at 718 Baltic Street, Apt. H, Seattle, Washington 98144.
The problems which I am having include the following:

    1. Broken toilet;

    2. Broken kitchen window;

    3. Leaky bedroom radiator;

    4. Crumbling plaster on
       livingroom ceiling.

I go to school in the mornings so please call me
between the hours of 1:00 p.m. and 5:00 p.m. and let me
know when you will be making your inspection. My
telephone number is 800-4231.

Sincerely,

B. Tenant

Request for inspection

you have already paid. Your landlord must return your damage deposit or security deposit if you are otherwise entitled to it.

If you are not covered by the Landlord-Tenant Act or if you are not current in rent or have not followed the procedures for giving notice, your landlord's failure to make repairs might still be considered a "constructive eviction" entitling you to move out (see page 79).

I. Rent Withholding

If your landlord doesn't make necessary repairs or provide necessary services, you may feel justified in not paying any rent. While withholding rent may seem like a good way to get your landlord's attention it can have some undesirable side effects which you should know about. There is no law which specifically permits you to withhold rent in Washington. Although it is not a crime to withhold your rent, a landlord could file a lawsuit to have you evicted for refusing to pay. You can be evicted even if you placed your rent in an escrow account or trust account.

The Washington Supreme Court has said that the only time a tenant can withhold rent completely is when it can be shown that the place being rented is totally uninhabitable.[18] If you are living in the place at the same time you are claiming that it is totally uninhabitable, a judge or jury is probably going to find that total rent withholding is not justified. You may be justified in refusing to pay part of the rent if you can show that the place is partially uninhabitable. However, partial rent withholding can be as risky as total rent withholding. If your landlord tries to evict you for not paying the full rent and a judge agrees that you didn't pay as much as you should have, you will generally not be given an opportunity to make up the difference and you will be evicted. You may also be liable for your landlord's court costs and attorney's fees.

August 24, 1977

J. Landlord
1434 Park Place
Seattle, WA 98104

Dear J. Landlord:

On July 21, 1977, I sent you a written notice to
repair describing the problems in my apartment at 718
Baltic Street, Apt. H, Seattle, Washington 98144.
Although more than thirty days have passed, you have not
started making any of the necessary repairs.

In accordance with the Landlord-Tenant Act, RCW
59.18.090, I am advising you that I am vacating my
apartment today due to your failure to make repairs
within a reasonable period of time. I paid you rent
in the amount of $90.00 on August 1, 1977, and am,
therefore, entitled to a $21.00 refund for the month of
August.

You may forward my refund and security deposit
to 808 Rose Street, Seattle, Washington 98108.

Sincerely,

B. Tenant

Notice of immediate termination

6

Your Landlord's Liability for Damages

A. When Is Your Landlord Responsible for Damages?

Your landlord is obligated to keep your place safe and free from hazards. He is also required to make certain repairs. If he doesn't do these things and as a result you are injured or your property is lost or damaged, you may be able to hold your landlord responsible for the damage.[1] This is a complicated area of the law and it is a good idea to talk to a lawyer before taking any action on your own. Before you decide to sue your landlord for damages because you tripped on a broken stairway or because someone broke into your place and stole your stereo, you should ask yourself the following questions:

1. Was the loss or injury caused by a problem in or around the place I was renting?
2. Could the loss or injury have been avoided if the problem had not existed?
3. Did the landlord have a duty to take care of the problem?
4. Did the landlord know (or should he have known) about the problem and fail to fix it within a reasonable period of time?

If your answer to all of these questions is *yes* then you may be able to recover damages from your landlord for the injuries or losses which you suffered. Although it may be possible to hold your landlord responsible for damages caused by defects that he did not know about,[2] you will generally be required to show that he knew or should have known about the problem.

Until the passage of the Landlord-Tenant Act in 1973, landlords

were not responsible for most repairs. Under those circumstances it was difficult for tenants to hold their landlords responsible for damages.[3] The duties of landlords are now more extensive. Their obligation to make repairs and provide a livable place has increased the likelihood of recovering damages if they don't. In some states, landlords have been required to reimburse tenants whose property has been stolen or who have suffered injuries caused by criminal acts which might have been prevented had the landlord provided proper security for the building.[4]

B. Agreements Not to Hold Your Landlord Responsible for Damages

A landlord may try to avoid liability for damages by putting a clause in your lease or rental agreement that he won't be responsible for injuries or damages, even if they were caused by his negligence or the negligence of his employees. Such a provision is called an "exculpatory clause." The following is an example:

> EXAMPLE: That neither the Lessor, nor his Agent, shall be liable for any injury to Lessee, his family, guests or employees or any other person entering the premises or the building of which the demised [leased] premises are a part, nor shall the Lessor be liable for any negligence of the Lessor or his Agent.

A clause like this in a residential lease or rental agreement is unenforceable.[5] If the landlord intentionally includes it in a lease or rental agreement, and a suit becomes necessary, he can be held liable for damages and reasonable attorney's fees.

C. What Are Your Damages?

There are many kinds of damages that you can recover from your landlord if his negligence results in your injury. Damages are intended to compensate you for losses or injuries which you have suffered. For example, your landlord could be required to reimburse you for your medical expenses, lost wages, reduction in future earning power, and for the disability, pain, suffering, and inconvenience that you experience.[6] If your place is burglarized because your landlord didn't have an adequate lock on the door, you may be able to collect from your landlord for the value of any property that was stolen.

7

Your Right to Privacy

A. When Can Your Landlord Enter Your Place?

When you rent a place you have a right to live there without unnecessary intrusions from your landlord or his employees. The Landlord-Tenant Act states that your landlord must have your permission to enter your place except when there is an emergency (like a fire or broken water pipe) or when you have abandoned the place.[1] The landlord must get your permission each time he wants to enter. A clause in a residential lease or rental agreement which says that your landlord can enter without your permission is invalid.[2]

Although the Landlord-Tenant Act requires your landlord to get your permission, you can't unreasonably refuse to let him in. If you unreasonably withhold permission after he has given proper notice, you could be held responsible for any damages caused by your refusal. Unreasonable refusal may also relieve your landlord of the obligation to make repairs.[3]

Proper reasons for entry by your landlord include:

1. Inspecting the place to check for damage or repair problems;
2. Making necessary or agreed repairs, alterations, or improvements;
3. Supplying necessary or agreed services;
4. Showing the place to possible purchasers, workmen, contractors, or possible future tenants.

Even though your landlord has a right to enter your place if he has a good reason and gets permission, he can't abuse that right or use it to harass you. Frequent requests from the landlord to

come in and inspect your place could be considered abuse or harassment unless some good reason can be shown for the inspections. Your landlord can only enter your place at reasonable times and must give you at least two days' advance notice. The notice can be either oral or written. If there is an emergency or if it is impracticable to give two days' advance notice then he can enter with shorter notice. The Act does not give any examples of when it might be "impracticable" to give two days' advance notice. If there is a problem with your place that is not an emergency but should be taken care of right away, it might be impracticable to give two days' advance notice. Even though it might be inconvenient for your landlord to give you two days' notice of his intent to enter when he wants to show the building to a possible purchaser or show your place to a future tenant, it is not impracticable to do so and you can insist that he schedule those appointments with your right to privacy in mind. The landlord still has to get your permission to enter, even if he has given two days' advance notice. He can't come in if you object and he can't enter the place if you are not there, unless you have authorized him to do so.

B. What Can You Do about Unauthorized Entry?

If your landlord enters your place without your permission and there is no emergency and you have not abandoned the place, he may have committed either criminal trespass or some other crime. You can call the police and have them investigate.[4] It may also be possible to sue your landlord for trespass. Ordinarily you can only recover nominal damages from a trespasser unless you can show that some specific damage was caused by his unlawful entry.[5]

8

Moving Out

A. Terminating Your Tenancy

1. If You Have a Lease

If you are renting a place for a specific period of time, like six months or one year, your tenancy ordinarily ends when the period expires. You can move out at the end of the period without giving any notice. Although this is the general rule, it is a good idea to read your lease to make sure there is no provision which requires you to give advance notice of your intention to move. If you stay beyond your lease expiration date and your landlord continues to accept your rent, you become a month-to-month tenant. Thereafter your tenancy can be terminated like any other month-to-month tenancy. Before your lease expires, you and your landlord should decide whether you will continue as a tenant. If your landlord does not agree to enter into a new lease or let you remain on the premises as a month-to-month tenant, you should make other living arrangements before the end of the lease term.

2. If You Are a Month-to-Month Tenant

If you are renting a place on a month-to-month basis and want to move out, you must give your landlord *written* notice of your intention to terminate the tenancy at least twenty days before the end of the rental period.[1]

> EXAMPLE: You are a month-to-month tenant and your rental period is from the first of the month to the first of the following month. If you want to terminate your tenancy and move out before October 1, you must give your landlord written notice on or before September 10.

September 10, 1977

TO: J. Landlord
      1436 Park Place
      Seattle, WA 98104

      This notice is to let you know that I will be
moving out of my apartment at 718 Baltic Street,
Apartment H, Seattle, Washington, on September 30, 1977.
This notice is given to you as required by the Landlord-
Tenant Act, RCW 59.18.200.

                             Sincerely,

                             B. Tenant

Notice to terminate tenancy

You can hand the notice to your landlord or his agent or you can send it by regular mail. If you send the notice by mail, be sure to allow additional time so your landlord will receive it at least twenty days before the end of the rental period. Keep a copy of the notice for your own records. Remember that the notice period begins on the day after the notice is delivered.

B. Breaking Your Lease or Moving Out without Giving Proper Notice

1. Your Responsibility for Rent

If you move without giving proper notice or if you move before your lease expires, your landlord can hold you responsible for additional rent.[2] Your landlord must try to find another tenant to replace you as soon as he finds out that you have moved. If you know people who are interested in renting the place, you should have them call your landlord.

If you are a month-to-month tenant, you can be held responsible for the rent for either thirty days after the landlord discovers that you moved or thirty days after the next regular rental due date, whichever comes first. If your landlord finds another tenant before the thirty days are up, he can only hold you responsible for rent for the days the place was vacant.

> EXAMPLE: You are a month-to-month tenant and your rental period is from the first of the month to the first of the following month. You pay $90 per month for rent and rent is due on the first of the month. You move out on October 31 without giving any notice and your landlord discovers that you have moved on November 2. He is able to find another tenant at an agreed rental of $90 per month. The new tenant moves in on November 21 and pays $30 for the remainder of the month.

In this example, your landlord would have a claim against you for $60 for the twenty days in November that the place was vacant. If he couldn't find another tenant, he could hold you responsible for rent for the entire month of November.

If you have a lease and move out before the end of the term, you can be held responsible for additional rent plus the costs incurred by your landlord in finding a new tenant. If your landlord is unable to find another tenant you will owe rent for the rest of the term. If your landlord finds another tenant before your lease expires, you will only owe rent for the time the place was vacant. If the place was rerented at a lower rent, however, you will also owe the difference between your rent and the new tenant's rent for the remainder of the term.

EXAMPLE: If you break a one-year lease after four months and it takes your landlord two months to find another tenant, you may have to pay your landlord rent for the two months the place was vacant. In addition, if you were supposed to pay $200 per month under your lease, and the new tenants are only paying $175 per month, you may have to pay your landlord an additional $25 per month for the remaining six months of the lease.

Again, your landlord can't just let the place remain vacant after you move out. He must try to find a tenant to replace you at a fair rental. If your landlord doesn't make a reasonable effort to find a new tenant, he can only hold you responsible for rent for the amount of time it *should* have taken to rerent the place. Your landlord can recover court costs and reasonable attorney's fees if he sues you for breaking your lease.

2. If You Leave Personal Property Behind

If you are current in your rent when you move out and you leave personal property behind, your landlord should take care of it for a reasonable period of time.[3] However, it is *never* a good idea to leave your property behind. If it is lost, stolen, or destroyed, it may be difficult to hold your landlord responsible.

If you are behind in rent and indicate by your words or actions that you have abandoned your place, your landlord can go in without your consent and without advance notice and remove and store any personal property you have left there.[4] Abandonment involves completely giving up your place with an intention not to return. If your landlord takes your property and claims you have abandoned your place, you may have to sue him to get your property back. Your landlord will then be required to prove in court by clear and convincing evidence that you abandoned the place.[5]

If your landlord takes your property he must promptly mail to your last known address a notice which contains his name and address and the name and address of the place where the property is stored. If he intends to sell your property he must first send you a notice of the proposed sale. After waiting sixty days from the date you fell behind in rent, he can then sell your property.

SUBLEASE

1. Parties: The parties to this sublease are:

   Sublessor (landlord) _____and

   Sublessee [tenant(s)] _____

   _____.

2. Property: Sublessor subleases the following property to Sublessee:_____.

3. Length of the sublease: The term of this sublease
   shall begin on the ___ day of _____, 197___
   and end on the ___ day of _____, 197___.

4. Rent and utilities: Sublessee agrees to pay rent in
   the amount of $_____ per month, payable on the
   1st of every month.
   Sublessee agrees to pay for all utilites.

5. Damage deposit: Sublessor acknowledges receipt of
   a damage deposit of $_____, to be returned on
   _____, 197___, if the premises have
   not been damaged, except for normal wear and tear.
   The deposit shall be held in sublessor's savings
   account located at: _____.

6. Conditions and rules: Sublessee agrees to comply
   with all rules and conditions of the lease between
   sublessor and her landlord; _____.
   A copy of this lease is attached and incorporated
   into this sublease by reference.

   _____   _____
   Date   Sublessor

   _____   _____
   Date   Sublessee

Sublease agreement

The proceeds from the sale can be applied to the back rent, any other damages which your landlord is entitled to, and the costs of transporting and storing your property. If the proceeds from the sale are greater than the amount you owe your landlord, he has to hold onto the excess for one year from the date of the sale. He can keep the excess if you don't claim it within one year.

C. Subleasing

If you have a lease that has not expired, you may be able to rent your place to someone else for all or part of the lease term. This is called subleasing.[6] While you can ask for more or less rent than you pay, it will be your responsibility to see that your landlord receives the rent required under your lease with him. When you sublease you become the landlord of the person who rents your place. If repairs are needed, it will be your responsibility to make them or get your landlord to make them.

Subleasing does not relieve you of your responsibility under the lease with your landlord. If the person you sublease to fails to pay the rent, breaks any rules of the tenancy, damages the place, or refuses to move when the lease expires, your landlord can hold *you* responsible. If the sublease expires before your lease and your tenant fails to move out, it will be your responsibility to bring a lawsuit to evict your tenant.

A sublease should be in writing and signed by you and your tenant. You will be responsible for damage that your tenant does to the place, so it is a good idea to ask for a damage deposit. Remember that all the laws concerning deposits which apply to landlords will also apply to you. Before you sublease your place, check your lease agreement carefully. Most leases prohibit subleasing without written permission from the landlord.

9

Deposits

A. Introduction

Often a landlord will demand a fee or a deposit to protect himself in case the tenant damages the place, fails to clean the place properly when moving out, or fails to comply with one of the requirements in the rental agreement. This chapter discusses deposits generally, the legal restrictions on deposits, and what tenants should do if a landlord refuses to refund a deposit.

B. What Is the Deposit For?

The first thing you should do if your landlord asks for a deposit is to find out what the deposit is for and what the requirements are for getting the deposit back. Here is a list of some of the more common fees and deposits requested by landlords:

1. *Damage deposit*—to be applied towards any costs paid by your landlord to repair damage to the place done by you or your guests.

2. *Security deposit*—to be applied towards actual losses of your landlord that result from your failure to comply with the requirements in the rental agreement. For example, if you fail to pay rent as required under the rental agreement, your landlord can terminate your tenancy and deduct the unpaid rent from the security deposit.

3. *Cleaning fee*—to be applied towards the expenses of cleaning the place after you move out. Some landlords request a *nonrefundable cleaning fee*. This means that regardless of how clean you leave the place, the fee will not be refunded.

4. *Last month's rent paid in advance*—technically not a de-

posit but payment in advance of the rent for the last month you live in the place.

5. *Holding deposit*—to be paid by you in return for the landlord's promise not to rent the place to another person before you move in. Usually, this fee is forfeited if you change your mind and do not move in. If you do move in, this deposit is usually applied towards the first month's rent.

The label given to the deposit can be important if your landlord doesn't tell you what the requirements are for refunding it. In that case, both you and your landlord will probably be bound by the generally accepted restrictions on that particular type of deposit.

C. When Can Your Landlord Ask for a Deposit?

Usually your landlord will ask for a deposit before you move in. If you are a month-to-month tenant, however, your landlord can ask for a deposit, increase an existing deposit, or change the requirements for return of an existing deposit at any time as long as proper notice is given. Your landlord must give you written notice of the proposed change at least thirty days before the end of the rental period.[1] In Washington there is no limit on how much money your landlord can demand for a deposit.[2]

D. Requirements for Getting Your Deposit Back

Regardless of what the deposit is called, the requirements for getting it back depend on what the agreement was with your landlord when you paid it.

EXAMPLE: Your landlord calls your deposit a holding fee but he told you when you paid it that it would be refunded if you left the place clean. The deposit is really a cleaning fee and should be treated as one.

EXAMPLE: You paid a cleaning deposit but your landlord never told you exactly what you must do when you move to get it back. As long as you leave the place clean, except for normal wear and tear, your landlord must refund the deposit when you move.[3]

The Landlord-Tenant Act specifically requires your landlord to tell you in advance if a cleaning fee is nonrefundable and it prohibits your landlord from applying any refundable deposit towards cleaning or damage which is the result of normal wear and tear.[4]

The Act does not define normal wear and tear. If you and your landlord cannot agree on what constitutes normal wear and tear, you will have to sue to get back your deposit. Courts, using common sense, decide what constitutes normal wear and tear in each individual case.

E. Forfeiting Your Deposit

Some month-to-month rental agreements have a clause that the security deposit will be forfeited if you do not stay for a minimum term (usually six months). Unfortunately, there are no court cases in Washington which have considered whether this type of deposit clause is valid.[5]

Here are some arguments you can make to your landlord or to a judge if you do not feel you should have to forfeit your deposit because you did not stay for the minimum term:

1. If You Move because of Problems with Your Landlord

You may not want to stay for the minimum number of months because of problems with your landlord. For example, your landlord may have raised the rent after you moved in, he may have failed to make repairs, or perhaps the building was too noisy. It would be unfair to allow your landlord to keep your deposit when it was his fault that you moved before the minimum term had expired. A court can choose not to enforce a clause in a rental agreement if it is grossly unfair to one side.[6]

2. If You Move for Other Reasons

If your decision to move out early has nothing to do with your landlord, you still can make the argument that the clause is a penalty and should not be enforced by a judge. Clauses in a lease or rental agreement where one person (the tenant) agrees to give up a set sum of money (the deposit) to compensate the other person (the landlord) for any damages that result from violating one of the terms of the agreement (agreeing to stay at least six months) can be valid.[7] In order for this type of clause to be valid, the sum of money the tenant gives up must be a reasonable estimate of what the landlord's actual damages are likely to be. The actual damages also must be hard to estimate accurately. If the clause does not meet these two criteria, the clause is considered a penalty and courts ordinarily will not enforce a penalty.[8] A judge may decide that a deposit forfeiture clause in a rental agreement is a penalty. First, the sum to be given up frequently has no relationship to what the landlord's actual losses are likely to be. Often, the only expense that a landlord will have as a result of a tenant's moving within six months is the cost of advertising to find a new tenant. This expense should be much less than the average deposit of $50 or $100. Second, there is no reason why the actual damages to the landlord if a tenant moves out early should be hard to estimate accurately.

If you are suing in small claims court to recover your deposit, this legal argument can be difficult to make on your own. Also, be aware that there is no way of knowing if the judge will agree that in your particular case your deposit is, in fact, a penalty.

F. What Happens to Your Deposit during the Tenancy?

The Landlord-Tenant Act requires your landlord to give you a written receipt for your deposit. If you paid a refundable deposit, he must also give you written notice of the name, address, and location of the bank or escrow company where the money is deposited.[9] Unfortunately, the Landlord-Tenant Act does not provide any penalty if your landlord refuses to provide this information. The Landlord-Tenant Act also requires your landlord to put any refundable deposit in a bank or escrow account, located in this state. Your landlord may not use or spend deposit money while you are still living in your place. Again, there is no penalty in the Landlord-Tenant Act if your landlord refuses to put the money in a bank or escrow account. If the deposit is put in an interest bearing bank account, your landlord is entitled to the interest unless you and your landlord have a written agreement that you are to have the interest.

If your landlord sells the property while you are still living there, he must transfer the deposit to the buyer, who will be your new landlord. Your new landlord must then put the money in a bank or escrow account and give you notice of the name, address, and location of the new bank or escrow account where the deposit is placed. If there seems to be a dispute between your old landlord and your new landlord about who should refund your deposit, it is a good idea to sue both of them.

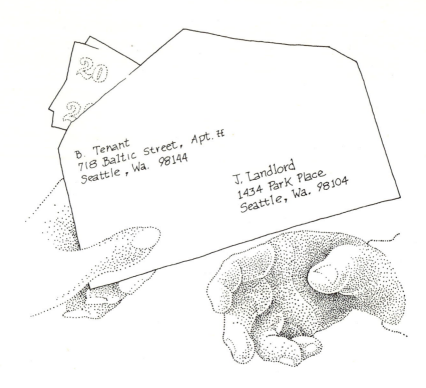

G. What Happens to Your Deposit when You Move?

Assuming that your deposit is refundable (depending on the original agreement with your landlord), your landlord is supposed to refund your deposit within *fourteen days* after you move or give you a statement itemizing why all or part of the deposit will not be refunded.[10] This notice is to be given to you personally or mailed to your present address. If your landlord does not have your present address then he can send it to the last address he is aware of (usually the place you just moved from). If your landlord fails to give you a notice within this fourteen-day period that he is keeping part or all of your deposit, the consequences are unclear. The Landlord-Tenant Act does not specifically provide for any penalty if a landlord fails to comply with the fourteen-day notice requirement. However, you can argue to your landlord or the court that if within fourteen days your deposit is not returned or you are not given notice why the deposit is being kept, you are entitled to the *entire* deposit regardless of whether the landlord can prove any damages. The fourteen-day limitation would be meaningless if landlords could ignore the notice requirements and still be entitled to keep the deposit.

Keep in mind that your deposit is *not* the maximum amount that you may have to pay your landlord if you damage the place. If your landlord does not feel that the deposit is enough to pay for his losses, he can sue you for the difference between your deposit and his actual out-of-pocket expenses. If your landlord sues you for the excess damages that were not covered by your deposit, the person who wins in court may have to pay the other person's attorney's fees.[11]

H. What to Do if Your Landlord Refuses to Refund Your Deposit

One of the most common problems for tenants is the landlord who refuses to refund all or part of a refundable deposit.[12] If your landlord has not refunded your deposit within fourteen days after you move out, first send him a letter demanding payment. If you do not get a satisfactory response to this letter, you will have to sue your landlord in order to recover your deposit. The Landlord-Tenant Act provides that the person who loses this lawsuit may have to pay the other person's attorney's fees and court costs.[13] If the lawsuit is filed in small claims court, attorney's fees usually are not applicable since in most cases neither side will be represented by an attorney.

If your deposit is less than $300, the quickest and easiest way to get your deposit back is to file your lawsuit in small claims court. Regardless of whether you sue in small claims court, district court, or superior court, the way in which you present your case will be very similar.

1. How to Present Your Case to the Judge

Since you are the person who filed the lawsuit, you will be the first one to tell your side of the story to the judge. Small claims court is very informal and the judge will frequently ask all of the questions. Here are some suggestions on how to present your case:

1. Briefly summarize the background facts of your case, such as:

September 15, 1977

J. Landlord
1434 Park Place
Seattle, WA 98104

Dear J. Landlord:

    I moved out of my apartment at 815 Atlantic
Street, Seattle, Washington, on August 31, 1977. I
left the place spotless when I moved.

    I have not yet received my cleaning deposit of
$50 from you. As I am sure you know, the Landlord-
Tenant Act requires you to refund deposits within
fourteen days after a tenant moves out. The Act also
provides that if I am forced to sue you to recover the
deposit, and I win, you may also have to pay my attorney's fees and court costs.

    Please mail my deposit of $50 to me immediately
at my new address: 718 Baltic Street, Apartment H,
Seattle, Washington 98144. If I do not receive this
check within one week, I will file a lawsuit to recover
the deposit.

                     Sincerely,

                     B. Tenant

Request for refund of deposit

(a) amount and type of deposit;

(b) requirements for refunding deposit;

(c) date you moved and condition of place when you left; and

(d) any notices received from your landlord stating why the deposit would be retained.

2. Tell the judge why you feel you should get your deposit back.

EXAMPLE: Your Honor, my landlord told me that I would get my deposit back if I left the place clean. When I moved out I thoroughly cleaned everything in the place.

3. Show the judge any evidence you have that is related to why you should get your deposit refunded. If you got a receipt when you paid the deposit, show it to the judge. If you have any other written agreement regarding the deposit, show that to the judge also. If the dispute is about the condition of the place, either when you moved in or out, show the judge any pictures you may have of the place.

4. After you tell your side of the story, you may call any witnesses you have who have some personal knowledge of the facts that are being disputed. Remember that your witnesses must come with you to court. Ordinarily the judge will not consider letters or notarized statements from your witnesses. Either you or the judge should ask the witnesses questions.

5. If there is anything in the Landlord-Tenant Act or in this handbook that you feel is relevant to why you should get your deposit back, show that to the judge also.

6. If your landlord disagrees with anything you or your witnesses tell the judge, he can ask you questions. It is important to answer the landlord's questions politely even if they are asked in a hostile or rude manner.

2. How Your Landlord Will Defend the Lawsuit

After you present your case to the judge, your landlord will then be allowed to tell his side of the story to the judge. He also can call witnesses to testify on his behalf and he can show the judge any evidence that is relevant to why he withheld your deposit. If you disagree with anything your landlord or his witnesses tell the judge, you can ask them questions.

When you sue your landlord, he can file a counterclaim if he feels that you owe *him* money. Frequently when a landlord is sued for a deposit, he will counterclaim for damages which he claims were the reason for not refunding the deposit in the first place.

EXAMPLE: You file a lawsuit to get back your $100 deposit. Your landlord files a counterclaim for $200 for rent he claims you did not pay for two months. If you win, you will get a judgment against your landlord for $100. If your landlord wins his counterclaim, however, he will get a judgment against you for $200. This means you will end up owing your landlord $100.

Before you decide to sue your landlord you should figure out whether you owe him any money. If you owe your landlord as much or more money than he owes you for your deposit, it probably will not accomplish anything to sue him. If your landlord files a counterclaim for damages but did not send you a statement within fourteen days telling you why he would not refund your deposit, you can make the argument that it is too late for him to now make this counterclaim.

10

Legal Evictions

A. Introduction

Once you have moved in, the *only* way your landlord can legally evict you is to file a lawsuit and get the judge to order the sheriff to evict you. It makes no difference why your landlord wants you to move out and it makes no difference what you have done. If you do not move out voluntarily, your landlord *must* go to court and ask the court to order the sheriff to evict you.

Your landlord cannot evict you by shutting off utilities, locking you out, taking your property, or just moving another tenant in. Chapter 11 discusses in more detail these illegal evictions. This chapter discusses how the court eviction procedure works and how you can defend yourself in court.

B. The Unlawful Detainer Lawsuit

Before your landlord can have you evicted by the sheriff he must file a lawsuit called an unlawful detainer action. The unlawful detainer action was especially created to provide landlords with a quick procedure to evict tenants.[1] While most lawsuits can take months or years to get to trial, unlawful detainer actions are usually tried within thirty days after they are filed.[2] In addition, unlawful detainer actions provide a procedure for evicting tenants before there is even a trial. To bring an unlawful detainer action landlords are required to follow the procedures contained in both the Unlawful Detainer Act and the Landlord-Tenant Act.[3]

An unlawful detainer action can only be filed against a tenant who is still living in the place. If a landlord files an unlawful detainer action against a tenant *after* the tenant has moved, the judge should dismiss the lawsuit.[4]

C. Eviction Notices

1. When Is an Eviction Notice Required?

Your landlord must give you a written eviction notice before he can begin an unlawful detainer action.[5] The only exception to this rule is if you have a lease and your lease has expired. In that case, if you do not move on the day your lease expires or get your landlord to agree to renew the lease, your landlord can start an unlawful detainer action without giving any notice at all.

If your landlord fails to give you an eviction notice before filing his lawsuit or if he gives the wrong notice, you should tell the judge. If the judge is convinced that you never received an eviction notice or that the notice you received was incorrect, then he should throw the lawsuit out.

2. How an Eviction Notice Is Served

Before your landlord can begin an unlawful detainer action he must first tell you that he wants you out, when he wants you out, and why. These notices, which will be explained in greater detail later, can be delivered to you ("served") in one of three ways:[6]

1. If you are at home, a copy of the notice must be left with you personally.
2. If you are not at home, one copy of the notice must be left with anyone at your house who can be expected to give it to you *and* a second copy must also be mailed to you.
3. If there is no one at home who can be personally served with the notice, then a copy of the notice must be attached to a conspicuous place on the property (like the door) *and* a second copy mailed to you.

3. Types of Eviction Notices

The required content of each type of eviction notice can be found in the Unlawful Detainer Act. The type of notice that you receive will depend on why your landlord wants to evict you. All notices must be in writing. The eviction notice will state how much time you have to move out before an unlawful detainer action can begin. When computing notice periods, do not count the day the notice is delivered and allow the full notice period following the date of delivery.[7]

EXAMPLE: You receive a three-day notice to pay rent or vacate on April 4th. You have April 5th, 6th, or 7th to pay your rent or move.

(Sample notices can be found at Appendix B, 1–4.)

a. *The three-day notice to pay rent or move out.* Before you can be evicted for not paying your rent, you must be given a three-day notice to pay the rent or move out. Your landlord can deliver the notice whenever the rent is overdue, even if it is only one day late. The notice must specify how much rent you owe and indicate that you have the choice of paying or moving within the three-day period.

If you offer your landlord all the rent owing within the three days allowed, he must accept it. He is not obligated to accept a partial payment, however. After the three days have passed he can refuse even full payment and can go ahead and file the unlawful detainer action. Keep in mind that even if you move out, you are still obligated to pay the rent you owed when you left.

Your landlord may accept the rent after the three-day period and attempt to evict you anyway. Therefore, whenever you offer rent after the three days have passed, be sure to get your landlord to agree in writing that he will not evict you after accepting your rent.

b. *The ten-day notice to comply with terms of the rental agreement or move out.* Whenever you fail to observe a rule or perform a duty required by your rental agreement your landlord can give you a ten-day notice to comply with the agreement or move out. If you do what the notice says, within the ten-day period, you cannot be evicted. If you fail to comply within the ten-day period, your landlord can begin an unlawful detainer action to have you evicted. The notice must clearly indicate that you have the choice of complying or moving out.

If your landlord accepts rent after the ten-day period has passed, he can no longer evict you for the reasons given in that ten-day notice.[8] He must serve another notice and wait until the ten-day period passes before starting an eviction action. If you comply with the second notice, you cannot be evicted.

c. *The three-day notice to move out for destroying property or creating a nuisance.* If you have destroyed your landlord's property or have created or kept a nuisance on the property, you may receive a three-day notice directing you to move out. Unlike the ten-day notice to comply with the rental agreement, this notice does not give you an opportunity to correct the violation. You must move within the three-day period or face eviction.

A nuisance, as the word is used here, is something that affects the livability of the place or the surrounding community.[9] A chicken coop in your apartment is a nuisance; a person who is merely obnoxious or annoying is not.

d. The three-day notice for trespassers. If you move into a place without the owner's permission, before you can be evicted you must be served a three-day notice ordering you to move out.[10] Keep in mind, however, that you can also be charged criminally with trespassing. If you offer to pay rent and the owner accepts it, you become a month-to-month tenant.

e. The twenty-day notice to terminate your tenancy. Unless you have a lease you can be asked to move at any time. It makes no difference how long you have lived there and it makes no difference that you were a model tenant. Your landlord does not have to give you any reasons for asking you to move. Before you can be evicted, however, you must be given a written notice, at least twenty days before the end of the rental period, telling you to move before the next rental period begins.[11]

> EXAMPLE: If you pay rent on the first of each month, your landlord must give you notice by the tenth of the month telling you to move before the first of the following month. (If there are thirty-one days in the month you must receive notice by the eleventh.)

If you receive fewer than twenty days notice, you cannot be required to move at the end of that rental period. A notice delivered on the fifteenth of the month, for example, could not end your tenancy on the thirtieth of the same month. You also cannot be required to move in the middle of a rental period. If your rent is due on the first of each month, you cannot be told on January 15 to move out by February 5. Once you have received proper notice, however, you must move out unless you can establish that the reason your landlord gave you the notice was either retaliatory or discriminatory.

D. The Court Papers in an Unlawful Detainer Action

1. The Summons and Complaint

After you have been served an eviction notice and have not obeyed its instructions, your landlord can begin an unlawful detainer action. The action is started by filing or serving a summons and complaint.[12] The summons and complaint will let you know that the lawsuit has been started. Until you have received the summons and complaint the court cannot lawfully order your eviction.

In most cases the summons and complaint are delivered together but they can be served separately. They can be delivered by anyone age eighteen or over who is not involved in the lawsuit. There is no requirement that the summons and complaint be delivered by the sheriff or any official.

The summons and complaint can be given to you personally anywhere: at work, at a neighbor's house, in a store, in a restaurant. If you are at home the summons and complaint should be given to you personally. If you are not at home or are unavailable when they are delivered, the papers can be left with anyone who lives with you who can reasonably be expected to give them to you (a person of suitable age and discretion). When the summons and complaint are delivered *do not refuse them*. You are properly served when the papers are presented to you or someone who lives with you, whether you accept them or not. By refusing the summons and complaint, you deny yourself the opportunity of defending the lawsuit.

An unlawful detainer summons must state that the suit is an unlawful detainer action and that your landlord wants you evicted.[13] It should give the date your response is due, which should be not less than six nor more than twelve days from the date the summons is served.[14] If your landlord does not serve an unlawful detainer summons the court should not allow him to use the quick unlawful detainer eviction procedure.[15]

The complaint is your landlord's written statement of why he thinks you should be evicted. Unlike the summons, the unlawful detainer complaint has no special form requirements. It must, however, state that an eviction notice was served and that you failed to obey it (unless you refused to move after your lease expired, in which case no notice is needed). If the complaint does not state that proper notice was served then the court should refuse to evict you.[16] Neither the summons nor the complaint that you receive need be signed by anyone to be valid. The original of both documents are signed and filed with the court. The copies that you receive may or may not show that the originals were signed. If you have any questions about the papers you receive or the service of those papers, *see a lawyer*. Never assume that any legal document you receive is invalid, no matter how you got it and no matter what it says.

2. *The Answer*
The answer is your response to your landlord's complaint. In it you (the defendant) admit or deny the statements made by your landlord (the plaintiff) in his complaint, and explain why you should not be evicted. You also describe any money claims that you have against your landlord.

On or before the date specified in the unlawful detainer summons, your written answer must be delivered both to the clerk of the court and to the person who represents your landlord, usually his attorney. You should first deliver a copy of your answer to your landlord's attorney. Ask him to write or stamp the words "copy received" and the date on the original of the answer. It is also a good idea to have him write or stamp "copy received" on your own personal copy of the answer. After delivering your written answer to your landlord's lawyer, file the original of the answer with the clerk of the superior court. Be sure to have the clerk stamp your copy.

When you take your answer to the court the clerk may tell you that it cannot be accepted because your landlord has not filed the unlawful detainer action. When this happens *do not* disregard the lawsuit. The unlawful detainer action can be filed at any time. If you have delivered a copy of your answer to your landlord's attorney, however, he is obligated to notify you when the action is filed. As soon as you are informed that the action has been filed, take the original of your answer and file it with the superior court clerk. It is extremely important to serve and file your answer on or before the response date on the summons. If you are even one day late your landlord can get a judgment by default for whatever he asked for in his complaint. The judgment will include not only an eviction order but also the amount of money your landlord claims you owe and his attorney's fees. Once a default judgment has been entered, it is extremely difficult, if not impossible, to set it aside. Even if there are many good reasons for your not being evicted, you may never get the opportunity to tell your story if you do not answer the unlawful detainer action in time.

3. Order to Show Cause

When you are served the summons and complaint you may receive an "order to show cause."[17] The order may also be delivered after you have received the summons and complaint. It will direct you to appear in court on a specific date, at a specific time, and tell the court why you should not be evicted *before* the trial. The date for the hearing should be not less than six nor more than twelve days from the date that you receive the order. *Do not disregard the order to show cause*. If you fail to appear at the hearing, an eviction order and possibly a judgment will be entered against you by default.

Although the summons and order to show cause are often delivered together and usually require a response on the same day, there is no requirement that the response dates be the same. In many cases the order to show cause will need a response before the summons. Occasionally, the summons will need the first response. You should examine both the summons and order to show cause very carefully and obey the instructions of each. The purposes and procedures of the show cause hearing are discussed below.

4. The Writ of Restitution

The writ of restitution is a paper, signed by a judge or court commissioner, ordering the sheriff to put you out.[18] Until the sheriff receives the writ there can be no eviction. The landlord can only get a writ of restitution after a trial, after a show cause hearing, or after you fail to answer or appear for a hearing within the time period specified on the summons or order to show cause.

E. What Happens in Court?

Once the necessary papers have been served and filed, a judge or jury will decide whether you should be evicted and whether a money judgment should be entered against you. The decision will be made after either a trial or a show cause hearing. Although the trial and the show cause hearing are similar in many respects, their rules and purposes are different. It is important to understand both the similarities and differences. The tenant who confuses them can get into serious trouble.

I. The Show Cause Hearing

a. The procedure. The primary purpose of the show cause hearing is to decide whether your landlord is entitled to have you evicted immediately or whether it is necessary to go through a trial.[19] The hearing is conducted by a judge or court commissioner. You and your landlord and any witnesses should be questioned, either formally or informally, to determine the facts of the case.

At the end of the hearing, the judge or commissioner decides whether you have any reasonable defenses to the eviction. If a reasonable defense is shown, the judge or commissioner should deny your landlord's request for immediate eviction and order that a full trial be held within thirty days. If, however, it is decided that your defenses are frivolous, a writ of restitution will be signed immediately.

If the judge or commissioner feels that you may possibly have a defense, but is not convinced of its merit, he or she will probably sign the writ of restitution and order that a trial be held to decide the merits of the defense. The case will be scheduled for trial like any other case. The length of time it takes for the case to come to trial will depend upon the number of cases pending in the superior court of the county in which you reside. In some counties it could take a year or more.

If the judge or court commissioner determines that you have no legal or factual defense to some of your landlord's claims, a final judgment will be entered against you as to those claims. If it is determined that you have no legal or factual defenses whatsoever, then a final judgment will be entered against you and there will not be a trial. It is very important, therefore, to come to the show cause hearing prepared to prove all your claims and defenses. Bring any witnesses, photographs, receipts, or other evidence which will support your story.

b. Bonds. A bond is a sum of money set aside to cover certain contingencies. When a writ of restitution is denied after a show cause hearing, neither you nor your landlord should be required to post a bond. When a writ of restitution is granted, however, the court should require your landlord to post a bond in an amount large enough to cover all of your relocation expenses.[20] If the judge or court commissioner does not require a bond, you should remind him of the requirement. After the trial, if the court finds that you should not have been evicted, you should be able to move back in and recover from the bond the money you spent moving out, the money you spent moving back in, and any other expenses caused by the pre-trial eviction. Sometimes it can be very difficult to recover these costs if no bond has been posted.

When a writ of restitution is issued after a show cause hearing you can prevent the pre-trial eviction by posting a bond in an amount which will be set by the court.[21] If you are being evicted for nonpayment of rent, the bond will be set in an amount equal to the rent you owe plus the landlord's anticipated costs and attorney's fees. You must also continue to pay your monthly rent to the court or your landlord until the lawsuit is concluded. The bond must be posted within three days of the date when you were served the writ of restitution.

2. The Trial

At the trial, a judge or jury decides whether you will be evicted. In addition, any money claims which you and your landlord have asserted will be decided. If you want a jury to decide your case, you must request one *before* you are assigned a trial date. You must also pay a jury fee ($25 for a six-person jury and $50 for a twelve-person jury). If you are indigent and cannot afford the jury fee, you can request that the court waive it.[22]

The discussion of the unlawful detainer trial which follows is greatly simplified. It is intended only to help you understand what happens at the trial. It should not be viewed as a manual on how to represent yourself in court. A trial is a complicated proceeding. Your landlord will be represented by an attorney who knows the problems and pitfalls of trial practice. While self-representation may be better than no representation at all, you should, if at all possible, get an attorney to represent you at the trial. If you try to represent yourself you will be at a very serious disadvantage.

On the day of the trial you should come to court with the witnesses, photographs, papers, and other evidence that will prove the statements made in your answer. It is your responsibility to prove that the statements made in your answer are true. Never rely upon your landlord, or his witnesses, to prove any part of your case. You should assume that the only support for your claims will come from the evidence you present.

The trial usually begins with an opening statement by each party. In the opening statements you and your landlord will each explain to the court what you intend to prove and why the court should rule in your favor. Your landlord will then present his case. He will probably testify himself and have witnesses testify on his behalf. He will also introduce documents in support of his claims. After each of his witnesses testify you will be given an opportunity to question (cross-examine) them about their testimony.

When your landlord has presented his case you will be called upon to present yours. Before calling your first witness, state to the court in plain, simple language what you intend to prove and why you should not be evicted. When you complete your statement call your first witness. The questions that you intend to ask each witness should be prepared in advance. Remember that you will probably be your most important witness. Be prepared to tell your story under oath and answer your landlord's attorney's questions on cross-examination. After each of your witnesses completes his or her testimony, your landlord's attorney will cross-examine. When the cross-examination is completed you can question your witness again to clear up any confusion or misimpressions. When all of your witnesses have testified and all your papers have been presented, tell the judge that you rest your case. The judge will then ask for closing arguments. In your closing argument tell the court what you have proved and how you proved it and explain why the court should rule in your favor.

3. *The Judgment*

The court's final decision is called the judgment. If you lose, the judgment will direct that you be evicted and specify the amount of money you owe your landlord. The money judgment will be for rent owing, any money your landlord lost because you refused to move, court costs, and, in most cases, attorney's fees.[23]

If you have a lease which has not expired, and you have been

evicted for not paying your rent, you may be able to stay in your place even though the court has ordered that you be evicted. In order to avoid eviction, you must pay your landlord the amount of the judgment plus any court costs within five days after the judgment is signed.[24]

If you win at trial after having been evicted at the show cause hearing, you should be able to move back in. You can recover your moving expenses from the bond your landlord posted after the show cause hearing. The judgment will also specify the amount of money, if any, that your landlord owes on any money claims asserted in your answer and how much he should pay on your attorney's fees.[25]

4. The Sheriff's Eviction Procedure

When a writ of restitution is signed by a judge or court commissioner after a show cause hearing or trial, it is immediately taken to the sheriff. When the sheriff receives it he is required to send you a copy as soon as possible.[26] In addition to a copy of the writ of restitution, the sheriff will send a notice stating when the eviction will take place. The sheriff cannot evict you until three days after the writ is delivered. He must evict you, however, within ten days after the writ is signed. If you are still on the premises when the sheriff arrives, you and your belongings will be physically removed. By resisting the sheriff you subject yourself to criminal prosecution.

F. Should You Defend the Lawsuit?

Defenses to an unlawful detainer action are any reasons or explanations you can give to prevent your landlord from getting an eviction order or money judgment. A set-off is a claim for money your landlord owes you. Both defenses and set-offs should be asserted in your answer to your landlord's complaint (see pages 72–75).

When you receive the summons and complaint you should immediately decide whether you have any defenses or set-offs. Contesting an unlawful detainer action with no defenses or set-offs is hopeless and will result in your paying substantially higher attorney's fees and court costs to your landlord. Even if you do have defenses or set-offs, deciding whether to defend yourself against an unlawful detainer action is a difficult task. You must not only weigh the merits of your own claims and defenses but also decide whether the probable result is worth the time and expense. Even people who are thoroughly familiar with the law and the legal system sometimes have difficulty making this decision. If you possibly can, therefore, you should consult a lawyer before finally deciding on a course of action. The defenses that can be asserted in an unlawful detainer action are discussed in the following sections.

1. Factual Defenses

To get a judge to evict you or enter a money judgment against you, your landlord must make statements in his complaint and prove that they are true.

> EXAMPLE: If your landlord attempts to evict you for nonpayment of rent and you can prove that your rent was paid, you have a good factual defense. If your landlord bases his eviction on your failure to comply with a ten-day notice and you can show that you did comply with the terms of your rental agreement within ten days, you once again have a good factual defense.

Some common factual defenses are based on whether the person who files the unlawful detainer action is entitled to possession of the property,[27] whether the property has been destroyed or a nuisance permitted on the property, or whether you are a tenant for a fixed term or a month-to-month tenant. Minor mistakes in the complaint, such as misspelled names or incorrect dates or apartment numbers, are generally not legitimate defenses.[28]

2. Procedural Defenses

A procedural defense to an unlawful detainer action is a claim that your landlord failed to correctly follow one or more of the steps in the eviction procedure. Examples of procedural defenses include:

1. Your landlord's failure to serve an eviction notice.
2. Your landlord's failure to serve the *proper* eviction notice.
3. Your landlord's failure to serve an unlawful detainer summons.
4. The service of an unlawful detainer complaint after you move out.[29]

5. Your landlord's failure to serve the summons and complaint as required by law.

If the judge accepts your procedural defense, your landlord will be required to correct the mistake, which may mean starting all over again. Once the mistake has been corrected, however, you may be evicted unless you have some other defense to the lawsuit.

3. Other Defenses

a. *Habitability.* Your landlord is obligated to keep your place in a livable condition. In an eviction action based upon nonpayment of rent you may have a defense if you stopped paying all or part of your rent because your landlord had not made needed repairs. A judge who finds that your place is partially or totally uninhabitable can decide that the rent you should have paid is less than the amount that you agreed to pay. If the rent you paid was equal to or greater than the amount you should have paid then you will not be evicted.[30] Even if you believe that your place is partially or totally uninhabitable you cannot know in advance how much your total rental obligation will be reduced by a judge. If you withhold more rent than the judge thinks justified, you can be evicted for failure to pay the difference. To justify withholding all your rent you must prove that your place was totally uninhabitable. That is a difficult argument to make if you, in fact, lived there. You may be justified in withholding a full month's rent, however, if you can prove that your place has been partially uninhabitable for a long time.

This defense should not be approached lightly. The court will demand convincing proof of serious repair problems. Witnesses, photographs, building reports, and a well-planned presentation are essential for success at trial.

b. *Discrimination.* State law prohibits discrimination against tenants on the basis of sex, marital status, race, creed, color, or national origin. If you feel that your tenancy is being terminated for discriminatory reasons, including failure to comply with a discriminatory rule, regulation, or rent increase, you can claim discrimination as a defense to an unlawful detainer action.[31] City and county ordinances may prohibit discrimination against additional groups of people not protected by state law.

c. *Retaliation.* Your landlord cannot increase your rent, reduce your services, or increase your duties as a tenant because you asserted your rights under the Landlord-Tenant Act or complained to a governmental agency about conditions in your building.[32] Unfortunately, if you are a month-to-month tenant, the Act *does* allow your landlord to give you a twenty-day notice to terminate your tenancy for retaliatory reasons.

> EXAMPLE: You give your landlord a notice to make certain repairs, as provided in the Landlord-Tenant Act. Rather than comply with his duty to make the requested repairs, your landlord gives you a notice to move out in twenty days. This is a retaliatory eviction and it is *not* prohibited by the Landlord-Tenant Act.

If you feel that your landlord terminated your tenancy for retaliatory reasons you may still be able to assert retaliation as a defense to an unlawful detainer action. You should explain to the court that the protections for tenants in the Landlord-Tenant Act are meaningless if landlords can evict any tenant who tries to use these protections. Courts in other states have refused to evict tenants who were being evicted for retaliatory reasons.[33] You may also be able to assert retaliation as a defense if your landlord is trying to evict you because you organized other tenants or because you complained about your landlord's conduct to other persons or government agencies.

If you exercise your rights as a tenant and your landlord increases your rent or your obligations as a tenant within ninety days, then *he* must convince the judge that his action was not retaliatory. After the ninety-day period, however, *you* must convince the judge that your landlord's action was retaliatory. If you make a complaint to a government agency within ninety days *after* your landlord has increased your rent or your duties as a tenant, then *you* must convince the court that your complaint was made in good faith.

4. Set-offs

If your landlord owes you money, the Landlord-Tenant Act may allow you to claim that money in an unlawful detainer action.[34] This claim, called a set-off, has only two restrictions:

1. Your landlord must be seeking money from you in his unlawful detainer complaint.

2. Your claim must have something to do with the tenancy.
EXAMPLE: Your landlord is evicting you for failure to pay $50 rent. You had to pay a $50 electricity bill which should have been paid by your landlord. Your claim for $50 can be asserted as a set-off.
An example of a debt which cannot be asserted as a set-off is a claim for the $200 your landlord owes you for repairs you made on his car. The claim cannot be asserted because it has nothing to do with your tenancy.

If the unlawful detainer action is based on your failure to pay rent and if the judge decides that your landlord owes you more money than you owe your landlord, you should not be evicted for failure to pay the rent. You may also assert a set-off in other unlawful detainer actions that are not based on your failure to pay rent. While the set-off will not be a defense to the unlawful detainer action, it may reduce the amount of money you owe your landlord.

11

Illegal Evictions

A. Introduction

The only legal way that a landlord can evict a tenant is through the court procedure described in chapter 10. Any other methods such as lockouts, utility shutoffs, or taking personal property are unlawful.[1] In order to avoid the delay and expense of filing a lawsuit, landlords occasionally use unlawful methods to evict tenants. The most common types of illegal evictions are discussed below.

B. Lockouts

1. What Is a Lockout?

Instead of going through the legal eviction procedure, your landlord may padlock the door, change the locks, or attach a device to the doorknob that makes it impossible to use your key. No matter what your lease or rental agreement says and no matter how far behind you are in rent, lockouts and evictions by anyone but the sheriff are *always* illegal.

2. What Can You Do if You Are Locked Out?

If your landlord has locked you out, you have no obligation to return, even if you have a lease that hasn't expired.[2] If you want to get back in, however, you are entitled to do so. To get back in you will probably have to file a lawsuit and it could take several days or even weeks before you are actually able to return to your place. Any expenses caused by the lockout can be recovered from your landlord, including your court costs and attorney's fees if a lawsuit

is necessary.[3] If lockouts are prohibited by a local ordinance, the police may be able to help you get back in. Police assistance is discussed on page 80.

C. Taking Your Personal Property

1. When Can Your Landlord Take Your Property?

Unless you have abandoned your place and are behind in your rent, your landlord has no right to remove any of your personal belongings without your specific consent.[4] Even if you have not paid the rent and have violated the rental agreement, your landlord is prohibited from taking your personal property. Any clause in your rental agreement that gives him the authority to take your property is void.[5]

2. How Can You Get Your Property Back?

If your property is taken, first see if the police can help you get it back. Police assistance in these situations is discussed on page 80. If the police can't help you and your landlord refuses to return the property, you will probably have to sue to get it back. You should immediately deliver a written demand to your landlord that your property be returned. If your landlord does not promptly return your property, you can sue for the property itself or you can sue for whatever it will cost you to replace it. In either case, if you win you can recover your court costs and attorney's fees from your landlord.[6] If you sue to get the property back, the Landlord-Tenant Act provides a method for getting the property quickly, before trial, without posting a bond.[7]

D. Utility Shutoffs

1. When Is a Shutoff Illegal?

Your landlord can only shut off your gas, water, heat, or electricity to make necessary repairs. Any other intentional termination of utilities is illegal.[8] If you have not paid your utility bill, only the utility company can discontinue your service. Your landlord has no right to cut off your service even if he pays utilities and you have not paid the rent. If he intentionally stops paying the bill and the utility company discontinues service, his failure to pay should be treated as an intentional utility termination.[9] If the utility shutoff makes your place unlivable, it could amount to a "constructive eviction" and you would be free to move. (Constructive evictions are discussed in more detail below.)

2. What You Can Do about Utility Shutoffs

If any utility has been shut off, contact your landlord or building manager immediately. You may find that the break in service is unintentional. If the shutoff was improper you should try to convince your landlord or building manager to restore service. If discussions with the landlord don't get results, contact the utility company. Sometimes they can restore service quickly. If the utility company can't help, it may be necessary to file a lawsuit. The primary purpose of a lawsuit will be to have the utility turned back on. You can also get money damages for any loss you suffered because of the termination (like food spoiling in your freezer) and a penalty of up to $100 per day for each day that you were without service. Your landlord can also be required to pay your attorney's fees and court costs.[10]

Like lockouts and the taking of personal property, utility shutoffs may violate a local ordinance. If so, the police may be able to help you get your landlord to restore service.

E. Constructive Eviction

1. What Is a Constructive Eviction?

When a tenant is forced to move out of a place because the landlord creates a problem or allows a problem to continue that makes the place unlivable, it is called a "constructive eviction."[11] The most common constructive eviction arises from the landlord's failure to make repairs.[12] A constructive eviction can also result from your landlord's continued harassment.[13] Unlike the other illegal evictions and practices that have been discussed, constructive evictions are not necessarily intentional. They can result from your landlord's carelessness in not correcting problems which seriously interfere with your use of the property.

2. What You Should Do if You Are Constructively Evicted

To claim a constructive eviction you must show that you moved because it was impossible to continue living in your place. You do not need to give notice of your intention to move if your landlord knew about the problem for a reasonable period of time and failed to correct it.

Your obligation to pay rent ends on the day you move, even if you have an unexpired lease. In some circumstances, you are also entitled to a refund of any prepaid rent for that part of the month when you did not live there.[14] You can also recover from your landlord any expenses caused by your having to move.[15]

F. Help from the Police

If your landlord has illegally evicted you or is harassing you, it may be possible to get help from the police. Your landlord may be guilty of criminal trespass or burglary if he enters your place without your permission or takes your property.[16] The police, however, will not ordinarily get involved in landlord-tenant problems unless a crime has been committed.

In Seattle, lockouts, utility shutoffs, harassment, and other illegal evictions are prohibited by the Seattle Housing Code. By dialing 911, a Seattle tenant who has been locked out can summon a police officer.[17] In some circumstances the officer is empowered to arrest the owner or manager. In other cases the officer can issue a citation directing the owner or manager to appear in court and show why he should not be jailed or fined. Should the officer choose not to arrest or issue a citation, a tenant can file an in-person complaint against the landlord by filing a claim at the Seattle Police Department patrol clerk's desk on the third floor of the Public Safety Building. The claim will be processed by the police department and the corporation counsel (the city's lawyer) and can result in prosecution of the offending landlord.

The community service officers of the Seattle Police Department will also assist tenants who have been locked out. They do not have the power to make an arrest or issue citations, but through persuasion and the implied threat of actual police involvement, they can sometimes convince landlords to let tenants back into their houses or apartments.

Police procedures on landlord-tenant disputes vary from city to city and county to county. You should check to see if there are criminal penalties for illegal evictions or harassment where you live.

G. Help from the Attorney General

The Washington State Consumer Protection Act is designed to protect consumers from unfair and deceptive business practices.[18] Although courts have not yet ruled on the issue, there is no reason to assume that the business of renting living space should be treated differently than other businesses. If your landlord has engaged in unfair or illegal practices like lockouts or utility shutoffs, you may have a claim under the Consumer Protection Act. It may be possible to obtain an injunction against your landlord along with triple damages up to $1000, and reasonable attorney's fees.[19] Written complaints should be filed with the Consumer Protection Division of the Washington State Attorney General's Office. You should also see if there is a city or county consumer protection department in your area. For example, Seattle has its own Department of Licenses and Consumer Affairs.

12

Discrimination

A. What Is Illegal Discrimination?

It is unlawful for a landlord to refuse to rent to a person or impose different rental terms because of a person's sex, marital status, race, creed, color, national origin, or because the person is handicapped.[1] It is important to understand that a landlord's actions may be unfair and unreasonable and still not be unlawful discrimination. In order to be unlawful, the discrimination must be based on your being a member of one of the groups or classes of people protected by an antidiscrimination statute or ordinance. It is not illegal for a landlord to refuse to rent to you because he does not like the shoes you are wearing. His decision might be arbitrary and unreasonable, but there is no law which prohibits discrimination based on shoe styles.

Landlords are free to treat individuals differently. You cannot prove illegal discrimination simply by showing that a landlord did something to you that he did not do to other people. In order to prove illegal discrimination you must show that the landlord treated you differently *because* you are a member of a group which is protected by antidiscrimination laws.

> EXAMPLE: A single woman, living in an apartment building in which all the tenants are single women, is the only tenant to receive an eviction notice. Although her different treatment may be unfair, it is not sex or marital status discrimination.

B. What to Do about Discrimination

If you have been denied rental housing because of discrimination you may be able to force the landlord to rent to you and, in

82

addition, get money damages and attorney's fees.[2] Unlawful discrimination is also a defense to an eviction (see page 73).[3] If you think you have been the victim of housing discrimination, you can do any of the following:

1. Start a lawsuit immediately.
2. File a complaint with the Fair Housing Section of the Department of Housing and Urban Development.[4]
3. File a complaint with the Washington State Human Rights Commission.[5]
4. File a complaint with your city human rights department if there is one.

No matter what you decide to do, it is important to act quickly. In most cases a discrimination complaint must be filed shortly after the discrimination takes place. If you do not file in time, you will lose your right to file your claim. There is no cost for filing a housing discrimination claim with a government agency and you do not need a lawyer. Once you contact the agency, its staff can provide you with helpful information on how to pursue your claim.

13

Small Claims Court

A. Introduction

Small claims court was set up to provide a quick and inexpensive place to settle legal disputes over small amounts of money. If your landlord will not return your damage deposit or if you think you have been paying too much rent because the landlord has not been making necessary repairs, you may want to consider filing a lawsuit in small claims court.

Each Washington county has one or more district courts and each district court has its own small claims department. In small claims court you can only sue for money and the maximum amount you can ask for is $300.[1] A small claims court cannot force your landlord to return personal property which he has illegally taken from you. Nor can it order your landlord to stop harassing you. If you want something other than a judgment for money, you will have to go to a different court than small claims court.

B. Starting the Lawsuit

The first requirement for a suit in small claims court is that you have to file the lawsuit in the small claims court district in which the person you are suing lives.[2] Once you have figured out the right district you have to appear personally before a district court employee and fill out and sign a claim form. The fee for filing the claim is $1.00. A hearing date will be set up when the claim is filed. The notice of claim which is going to be served on the defendant (your landlord) has to include your name and address, the defendant's name and address, a brief description of the type of claim you have against the defendant, the amount of money you are asking for, and the date the claim arose. The notice of small claim also includes the date of the hearing and a warning that if the defendant doesn't show up at the hearing a judgment will be entered against the defendant for the amount stated in your claim. A sample claim form is included in Appendix B.

C. Serving the Notice of Claim

The notice of small claim has to be served on the defendant no less than five days and no more than ten days before the day of the hearing. The notice of small claim has to be served by itself without any other paper. There are a number of ways you can serve the notice. If the sheriff serves the notice you will have to pay a fee of $1.00 plus a charge for mileage. If the notice is served by a professional process server, the charges will vary. If you win your case, the service fees plus the charge for filing the claim will be added to the judgment against the defendant. You can also serve the notice of small claim by certified or registered mail and if this method is used, you must get a return receipt signed by the defendant and file that with the court either at the hearing or before the hearing. You are not allowed to serve the notice on the defendant yourself, but you could have a friend or acquaintance do it as long as the person doing the serving is eighteen years of age or over and does not have any financial interest in the lawsuit.[3]

The person serving the notice must either hand it to the defendant personally or leave a copy at the defendant's residence by handing it to a person of suitable age who lives there also. The person delivering the notice has to fill out a sworn statement explaining when, where, and how the defendant was served. The statement is called an "affidavit of service" and should be filed with the court at the time of the hearing or before the hearing.[4] A sample affidavit of service is included in Appendix B. If the defendant is a corporation you can serve the papers on the president, secretary, cashier, or managing agent of the corporation or on the secretary, stenographer, or office assistant of one of those persons.[5] If you need information about a corporation or its officers you can contact the secretary of state in Olympia. The telephone number is (206) 753-7115.

D. Counterclaims

If your landlord (the defendant) also has a claim against you it can be put in writing and served on you as long as it meets the

same requirements as original claims. The defendant's claims are called counterclaims. Both your claim and any counterclaims of your landlord will usually be heard by a judge at the same time. You should check with your local small claims court on the procedure for presenting counterclaims, since they may vary from district to district. In Seattle, the defendant may serve a counterclaim on the plaintiff anytime before the trial. A sample counterclaim is included in Appendix B.

E. What Happens at the Hearing

If you show up at the hearing and the defendant does not and you can prove that the notice was properly served, then the judge or justice of the peace will enter a judgment against the defendant for the amount of the claim. If the defendant shows up at the hearing and you do not, your claim will be dismissed. Your claim will also be dismissed if neither you nor the defendant shows up or you were unable to correctly serve the defendant. If your claim is dismissed you will have to pay another filing fee and start all over again if you still want to sue your landlord.

If both you and the defendant show up, the court will listen to both sides of the dispute and make a decision. The hearing is usually informal. Neither side is allowed to have a lawyer or anyone else help them without the court's permission. Witnesses are permitted but not required. If you have any pictures, bills, or receipts or if the defendant has made any written statements which help your case, be sure to bring those to court and show them to the judge.

The judge will make a decision after hearing both sides of the case. A judgment can be entered against the defendant for the entire amount requested or just part of that amount. The judge can also decide in favor of the defendant and dismiss your case and give the defendant a money judgment against you if a counterclaim was presented.

F. Collecting Judgments

If you get a judgment against the defendant, you are the one who is going to have the responsibility for collecting it. The judge cannot throw a defendant in jail or force him or her to pay the judgment. If the defendant refuses to pay the judgment voluntarily, you have to follow certain procedures to collect the money. If the losing party does not pay the judgment within twenty days after it is entered, you can notify the court and the judge who held the hearing is supposed to prepare a statement showing when the judgment was entered, the amount, and an indication that it has not been paid. Once that statement has been filed with the district court you are allowed to use the collection procedures which the law permits.[6] If you get a judgment against your present landlord, you may be able to deduct the amount of the judgment from your rent.[7]

G. Appeals

If you file a suit in small claims court and lose or do not get as much as you think you should, the decision is final and you cannot appeal. You only get one chance to prove your claim and if you lose you are not allowed to sue on the same claim again. A defendant who loses can only appeal to superior court if the amount of the claim was $100 or more.

Appendix A

The Residential
Landlord-Tenant Act of 1973

Chapter 59.18 RCW
RESIDENTIAL LANDLORD–TENANT ACT

(Revised June 15, 1977 pursuant to the
Washington Supreme Court decision in cause
number 43879 entitled WASHINGTON
ASS'N. OF APARTMENT ASS'NS., INC.
vs. EVANS; 88 Wn. 2d. 563, which declared
invalid the fourteen item and section vetoes to
1973 Engrossed Substitute Senate Bill No.
2226; 1973 1st ex. sess., chapter 207. The
governor exercised his veto power by at-
tempting to excise parts of sections 6, 7, 8,
11, 19, 23, 24, 25, and 31 and all of sections
43 and 47. The vetoed matter is herein restored as parts of RCW 59.18.060, 59.18-
.070, 59.18.080, 59.18.110, 59.18.190,
59.18.230, 59.18.240, 59.18.250, 59.18.310;
and in new sections RCW 59.18.415 and
59.18.430.)

RCW 59.18.010 Short title. RCW 59.18.010 through
59.18.420 and 59.18.900 shall be known and may be
cited as the "Residential Landlord–Tenant Act of
1973", and shall constitute a new chapter in Title 59
RCW. [1973 1st ex.s. c 207 § 1.]

RCW 59.18.020 Rights and remedies——Obligation of good faith imposed. Every duty under this chapter and every act which must be performed as a condition precedent to the exercise of a right or remedy under this chapter imposes an obligation of good faith in its performance or enforcement. [1973 1st ex.s. c 207 § 2.]

RCW 59.18.030 Definitions. As used in this chapter:

(1) "Dwelling unit" is a structure or that part of a structure which is used as a home, residence, or sleeping place by one person or by two or more persons maintaining a common household, including but not limited to single family residences and units of multiplexes, apartment buildings, and mobile homes.

(2) "Landlord" means the owner, lessor, or sublessor of the dwelling unit or the property of which it is a part, and in addition means any person designated as representative of the landlord.

(3) "Person" means an individual, group of individuals, corporation, government, or governmental agency, business trust, estate, trust, partnership, or association, two or more persons having a joint or common interest, or any other legal or commercial entity.

(4) "Owner" means one or more persons, jointly or severally, in whom is vested:

(a) All or any part of the legal title to property; or

(b) All or part of the beneficial ownership, and a right to present use and enjoyment of the property.

(5) "Premises" means a dwelling unit, appurtenances thereto, grounds, and facilities held out for the use of tenants generally and any other area or facility which is held out for use by the tenant.

(6) "Rental agreement" means all agreements which establish or modify the terms, conditions, rules, regulations, or any other provisions concerning the use and occupancy of a dwelling unit.

(7) A "single family residence" is a structure maintained and used as a single dwelling unit. Notwithstanding that a dwelling unit shares one or more walls with another dwelling unit, it shall be deemed a single family residence if it has direct access to a street and shares neither heating facilities nor hot water equipment, nor any other essential facility or service, with any other dwelling unit.

(8) A "tenant" is any person who is entitled to occupy a dwelling unit primarily for living or dwelling purposes under a rental agreement.

(9) "Reasonable attorney's fees", where authorized in this chapter, means an amount to be determined including the following factors: The time and labor required, the novelty and difficulty of the questions involved, the skill requisite to perform the legal service properly, the fee customarily charged in the locality for similar legal services, the amount involved and the results obtained, and the experience, reputation and ability of the lawyer or lawyers performing the services. [1973 1st ex.s. c 207 § 3.]

RCW 59.18.040 Living arrangements exempted from chapter. The following living arrangements are not intended to be governed by the provisions of this chapter, unless established primarily to avoid its application, in which event the provisions of this chapter shall control:

(1) Residence at an institution, whether public or private, where residence is merely incidental to detention or the provision of medical, religious, educational, recreational, or similar services, including but not limited to correctional facilities, licensed nursing homes, monasteries and convents, and hospitals;

(2) Occupancy under a bona fide earnest money agreement to purchase, bona fide option to purchase, or contract of sale of the dwelling unit or the property of which it is a part, where the tenant is, or stands in the place of, the purchaser;

(3) Residence in a hotel, motel, or other transient lodging whose operation is defined in RCW 19.48.010;

(4) Rental agreements entered into pursuant to the provisions of chapter 47.12 RCW where occupancy is by an owner–condemnee and where such agreement does not violate the public policy of this state of ensuring decent, safe, and sanitary housing and is so certified by the consumer protection division of the attorney general's office;

(5) Rental agreements for the use of any single family residence which are incidental to leases or rentals entered into in connection with a lease of land to be used primarily for agricultural purposes;

(6) Rental agreements providing housing for seasonal agricultural employees while provided in conjunction with such employment;

(7) Rental agreements with the state of Washington, department of natural resources, on public lands governed by Title 79 RCW;

(8) Occupancy by an employee of a landlord whose right to occupy is conditioned upon employment in or about the premises. [1973 1st ex.s. c 207 § 4.]

RCW 59.18.050 Jurisdiction of district and superior courts. The district or superior courts of this state may exercise jurisdiction over any landlord or tenant with respect to any conduct in this state governed by this chapter or with respect to any claim arising from a transaction subject to this chapter within the respective jurisdictions of the district or superior courts as provided in Article IV, section 6 of the Constitution of the state of Washington. [1973 1st ex.s. c 207 § 5.]

RCW 59.18.060 Landlord——Duties. The landlord will at all times during the tenancy keep the premises fit for human habitation, and shall in particular:

(1) Maintain the premises to substantially comply with any applicable code, statute, ordinance, or regulation governing their maintenance or operation, which the legislative body enacting the applicable code, statute, ordinance or regulation could enforce as to the premises rented if such condition substantially endangers or impairs the health or safety of the tenant;

(2) Maintain the roofs, floors, walls, chimneys, fireplaces, foundations, and all other structural components in reasonably good repair so as to be usable and capable of resisting any and all normal forces and loads to which they may be subjected;

(3) Keep any shared or common areas reasonably clean, sanitary, and safe from defects increasing the hazards of fire or accident;

(4) Provide a reasonable program for the control of infestation by insects, rodents, and other pests at the initiation of the tenancy and, except in the case of a single family residence, control infestation during tenancy except where such infestation is caused by the tenant;

(5) Except where the condition is attributable to normal wear and tear, make repairs and arrangements necessary to put and keep the premises in as good condition as it by law or rental agreement should have been, at the commencement of the tenancy;

(6) Provide reasonably adequate locks and furnish keys to the tenant;

(7) Maintain all electrical, plumbing, heating, and other facilities and appliances supplied by him in reasonably good working order;

(8) Maintain the dwelling unit in reasonably weathertight condition;

(9) Except in the case of a single family residence, provide and maintain appropriate receptacles in common areas for the removal of ashes, rubbish, and garbage, incidental to the occupancy and arrange for the reasonable and regular removal of such waste;

(10) Except where the building is not equipped for the purpose, provide facilities adequate to supply heat and water and hot water as reasonably required by the tenant;

(11) Designate to the tenant the name and address of the person who is the landlord by a statement on the rental agreement or by a notice conspicuously posted on the premises. The tenant shall be notified immediately of any changes by certified mail or by an updated posting. If the person designated in this section does not reside in the state where the premises are located, there shall also be designated a person who resides in the county who is authorized to act as an agent for the purposes of service of notices and process, and if no designation is made of a person to act as agent, then the person to whom rental payments are to be made shall be considered such agent.

No duty shall devolve upon the landlord to repair a defective condition under this section, nor shall any defense or remedy be available to the tenant under this chapter, where the defective condition complained of was caused by the conduct of such tenant, his family, invitee, or other person acting under his control, or where a tenant unreasonably fails to allow the landlord access to the property for purposes of repair. When the duty imposed by subsection (1) of this section is incompatible with and greater than the duty imposed by any other provisions of this section, the landlord's duty shall be determined pursuant to subsection (1) of this section. [1973 1st ex.s. c 207 § 6.]

RCW 59.18.070 Landlord——Failure to perform duties——Notice from tenant——Contents——Time limits for landlord's remedial action. If at any time during the tenancy the landlord fails to carry out the duties required by RCW 59.18.060, the tenant may, in addition to pursuit of remedies otherwise provided him by law, deliver written notice to the person designated in subsection (11) of RCW 59.18.060, or to the person who collects the rent, which notice shall specify the premises involved, the name of the owner, if known, and the nature of the defective condition. For the purposes of this chapter, a reasonable time for the landlord to commence remedial action after receipt of such notice by the tenant shall be, except where circumstances are beyond the landlord's control:

(1) Not more than twenty-four hours, where the defective condition deprives the tenant of water or heat or is imminently hazardous to life;

(2) Not more than forty-eight hours, where the landlord fails to provide hot water or electricity;

(3) Subject to the provisions of subsections (1) and (2) of this section, not more than seven days in the case of a repair under RCW 59.18.100(3);

(4) Not more than thirty days in all other cases.

In each instance the burden shall be on the landlord to see that remedial work under this section is completed with reasonable promptness.

Where circumstances beyond the landlord's control, including the availability of financing, prevent him from complying with the time limitations set forth in this section, he shall endeavor to remedy the defective condition with all reasonable speed. [1973 1st ex.s. c 207 § 7.]

RCW 59.18.080 Payment of rent condition to exercising remedies——Exceptions. The tenant shall be current in the payment of rent including all utilities which the tenant has agreed in the rental agreement to pay before exercising any of the remedies accorded him under the provisions of this chapter: *Provided,* That this section shall not be construed as limiting the tenant's civil remedies for negligent or intentional damages: *Provided further,* That this section shall not be construed as limiting the tenant's right in an unlawful detainer proceeding to raise the defense that there is no rent due and owing. [1973 1st ex.s. c 207 § 8.]

RCW 59.18.090 Landlord's failure to remedy defective condition——Tenant's choice of actions. If, after receipt of written notice, and expiration of the applicable period of time, as provided in RCW 59.18.070, the landlord fails to remedy the defective condition within a reasonable time the tenant may:

(1) Terminate the rental agreement and quit the premises upon written notice to the landlord without further obligation under the rental agreement, in which case he shall be discharged from payment of rent for any period following the quitting date, and shall be entitled

to a pro rata refund of any prepaid rent, and shall receive a full and specific statement of the basis for retaining any of the deposit together with any refund due in accordance with RCW 59.18.280;

(2) Bring an action in an appropriate court, or at arbitration if so agreed, for any remedy provided under this chapter or otherwise provided by law; or

(3) Pursue other remedies available under this chapter. [1973 1st ex.s. c 207 § 9.]

RCW 59.18.100   Landlord's failure to carry out duties——Repairs effected by tenant——Bids——Notice——Deduction of cost from rent——Limitations. (1) If at any time during the tenancy, the landlord fails to carry out any of the duties imposed by RCW 59.18.060, and notice of the defect is given to the landlord pursuant to RCW 59.18.070, the tenant may submit to the landlord or his designated agent by certified mail or in person at least two bids to perform the repairs necessary to correct the defective condition from licensed or registered persons, or if no licensing or registration requirement applies to the type of work to be performed, from responsible persons capable of performing such repairs. Such bids may be submitted to the landlord at the same time as notice is given pursuant to RCW 59.18.070: *Provided*, That the remedy provided in this section shall not be available for a landlord's failure to carry out the duties in subsections (6), (9), and (11) of RCW 59.18.060.

(2) If the landlord fails to commence repair of the defective condition within a reasonable time after receipt of notice from the tenant, the tenant may contract with the person submitting the lowest bid to make the repair, and upon the completion of the repair and an opportunity for inspection by the landlord or his designated agent, the tenant may deduct the cost of repair from the rent in an amount not to exceed the sum expressed in dollars representing one month's rental of the tenant's unit in any twelve-month period: *Provided*, That when the landlord must commence to remedy the defective condition within thirty days as provided in subsection (4) of RCW 59.18.070, the tenant cannot contract for repairs for at least fifteen days following receipt of said bids by the landlord: *Provided further*, That the total costs of repairs deducted in any twelve-month period under this subsection shall not exceed the sum expressed in dollars representing one month's rental of the tenant's unit.

(3) If the landlord fails to carry out the duties imposed by RCW 59.18.060 within a reasonable time, and if the cost of repair does not exceed one-half month's rent, including the cost of materials and labor, which shall be computed at the prevailing rate in the community for the performance of such work, and if repair of the condition need not by law be performed only by licensed or registered persons, the tenant may repair the defective condition in a workmanlike manner and upon completion of the repair and an opportunity for inspection, the tenant may deduct the cost of repair from the rent: *Provided*, That repairs under this subsection are limited to defects within the leased premises: *Provided further*, That the total costs of repairs deducted in any

twelve-month period under this subsection shall not exceed one-half month's rent of the unit or seventy-five dollars in any twelve-month period, whichever is the lesser.

(4) The provisions of this section shall not:

(a) Create a relationship of employer and employee between landlord and tenant; or

(b) Create liability under the workmen's compensation act; or

(c) Constitute the tenant as an agent of the landlord for the purposes of RCW 60.04.010 and 60.04.040.

(5) Any repair work performed under the provisions of this section shall comply with the requirements imposed by any applicable code, statute, ordinance, or regulation. A landlord whose property is damaged because of repairs performed in a negligent manner may recover the actual damages in an action against the tenant.

(6) Nothing in this section shall prevent the tenant from agreeing with the landlord to undertake the repairs himself in return for cash payment or a reasonable reduction in rent, the agreement thereof to be agreed upon between the parties, and such agreement does not alter the landlord's obligations under this chapter. [1973 1st ex.s. c 207 § 10.]

RCW 59.18.110   Failure of landlord to carry out duties——Determination by court or arbitrator——Judgment against landlord for diminished rental value and repair costs——Enforcement of judgment——Reduction in rent under certain conditions. (1) If a court or an arbitrator determines that:

(a) A landlord has failed to carry out a duty or duties imposed by RCW 59.18.060; and

(b) A reasonable time has passed for the landlord to remedy the defective condition following notice to the landlord in accordance with RCW 59.18.070 or such other time as may be allotted by the court or arbitrator; the court or arbitrator may determine the diminution in rental value of the premises due to the defective condition and shall render judgment against the landlord for the rent paid in excess of such diminished rental value from the time of notice of such defect to the time of decision and any costs of repair done pursuant to RCW 59.18.100 for which no deduction has been previously made. Such decisions may be enforced as other judgments at law and shall be available to the tenant as a set-off against any existing or subsequent claims of the landlord.

The court or arbitrator may also authorize the tenant to make or contract to make further corrective repairs: *Provided*, That the court specifies a time period in which the landlord may make such repairs before the tenant may commence or contract for such repairs: *Provided further*, That such repairs shall not exceed the sum expressed in dollars representing one month's rental of the tenant's unit in any one calendar year.

(2) The tenant shall not be obligated to pay rent in excess of the diminished rental value of the premises until such defect or defects are corrected by the landlord or until the court or arbitrator determines otherwise. [1973 1st ex.s. c 207 § 11.]

RCW 59.18.120 Defective condition——Unfeasible to remedy defect——Termination of tenancy. If a court or arbitrator determines a defective condition as described in RCW 59.18.060 to be so substantial that it is unfeasible for the landlord to remedy the defect within the time allotted by RCW 59.18.070, and that the tenant should not remain in the dwelling unit in its defective condition, the court or arbitrator may authorize the termination of the tenancy: *Provided*, That the court or arbitrator shall set a reasonable time for the tenant to vacate the premises. [1973 1st ex.s. c 207 § 12.]

RCW 59.18.130 Duties of tenant. Each tenant shall pay the rental amount at such times and in such amounts as provided for in the rental agreement or as otherwise provided by law and comply with all obligations imposed upon tenants by applicable provisions of all municipal, county, and state codes, statutes, ordinances, and regulations, and in addition shall:

(1) Keep that part of the premises which he occupies and uses as clean and sanitary as the conditions of the premises permit;

(2) Properly dispose from his dwelling unit all rubbish, garbage, and other organic or flammable waste, in a clean and sanitary manner at reasonable and regular intervals, and assume all costs of extermination and fumigation for infestation caused by the tenant;

(3) Properly use and operate all electrical, gas, heating, plumbing and other fixtures and appliances supplied by the landlord;

(4) Not intentionally or negligently destroy, deface, damage, impair, or remove any part of the structure or dwelling, with the appurtenances thereto, including the facilities, equipment, furniture, furnishings, and appliances, or permit any member of his family, invitee, licensee, or any person under his control to do so;

(5) Not permit a nuisance or common waste; and

(6) Upon termination and vacation, restore the premises to their initial condition except for reasonable wear and tear or conditions caused by failure of the landlord to comply with his obligations under this chapter: *Provided*, That the tenant shall not be charged for normal cleaning if he has paid a nonrefundable cleaning fee. [1973 1st ex.s. c 207 § 13.]

RCW 59.18.140 Reasonable obligations or restrictions——Tenant's duty to conform. The tenant shall conform to all reasonable obligations or restrictions, whether denominated by the landlord as rules, rental agreement, rent, or otherwise, concerning the use, occupation, and maintenance of his dwelling unit, appurtenances thereto, and the property of which the dwelling unit is a part if such obligations and restrictions are not in violation of any of the terms of this chapter and are not otherwise contrary to law, and if such obligations and restrictions are brought to the attention of the tenant at the time of his initial occupancy of the dwelling unit and thus become part of the rental agreement. Except for termination of tenancy, after thirty days written notice to each tenant, a new rule of tenancy may become

effective upon completion of the term of the rental agreement or sooner upon mutual consent. [1973 1st ex.s. c 207 § 14.]

RCW 59.18.150 Landlord's right of entry——Purposes——Conditions. (1) The tenant shall not unreasonably withhold consent to the landlord to enter into the dwelling unit in order to inspect the premises, make necessary or agreed repairs, alterations, or improvements, supply necessary or agreed services, or exhibit the dwelling unit to prospective or actual purchasers, mortgagees, tenants, workmen, or contractors.

(2) The landlord may enter the dwelling unit without consent of the tenant in case of emergency or abandonment.

(3) The landlord shall not abuse the right of access or use it to harass the tenant. Except in the case of emergency or if it is impracticable to do so, the landlord shall give the tenant at least two days' notice of his intent to enter and shall enter only at reasonable times.

(4) The landlord has no other right of access except by court order, arbitrator or by consent of the tenant. [1973 1st ex.s. c 207 § 15.]

RCW 59.18.160 Landlord's remedies if tenant fails to remedy defective condition. If, after receipt of written notice, as provided in RCW 59.18.170, the tenant fails to remedy the defective condition within a reasonable time, the landlord may:

(1) Bring an action in an appropriate court, or at arbitration if so agreed for any remedy provided under this chapter or otherwise provided by law; or

(2) Pursue other remedies available under this chapter. [1973 1st ex.s. c 207 § 16.]

RCW 59.18.170 Landlord to give notice if tenant fails to carry out duties. If at any time during the tenancy the tenant fails to carry out the duties required by RCW 59.18.130 or 59.18.140, the landlord may, in addition to pursuit of remedies otherwise provided by law, give written notice to the tenant of said failure, which notice shall specify the nature of the failure. [1973 1st ex.s. c 207 § 17.]

RCW 59.18.180 Tenant's failure to comply with statutory duties——Landlord to give tenant written notice of noncompliance——Landlord's remedies. If the tenant fails to comply with any portion of RCW 59.18-.130 or 59.18.140, and such noncompliance can substantially affect the health and safety of the tenant or other tenants, or substantially increase the hazards of fire or accident that can be remedied by repair, replacement of a damaged item, or cleaning, the tenant shall comply within thirty days after written notice by the landlord specifying the noncompliance, or, in the case of emergency as promptly as conditions require. If the tenant fails to remedy the noncompliance within that period the landlord may enter the dwelling unit and cause the work to be done and submit an itemized bill of the actual and reasonable cost of repair, to be payable on the next date when periodic rent is due, or on terms mutually agreed to by the landlord and tenant, or immediately if the rental agreement has terminated. Any substantial noncompliance by the tenant of RCW 59.18.130 or 59.18-.140 shall constitute a ground for commencing an action in unlawful detainer in accordance with the provisions of chapter 59.12 RCW, and a landlord may commence such action at any time after written notice pursuant to such chapter. The tenant shall have a defense to an unlawful detainer action filed solely on this ground if it is determined at the hearing authorized under the provisions of chapter 59.12 RCW that the tenant is in substantial compliance with the provisions of this section, or if the tenant remedies the noncomplying condition within the thirty day period provided for above or any shorter period determined at the hearing to have been required because of an emergency: *Provided,* That if the defective condition is remedied after the commencement of an unlawful detainer action, the tenant may be liable to the landlord for statutory costs and reasonable attorney's fees. [1973 1st ex.s. c 207 § 18.]

RCW 59.18.190   Notice to tenant to remedy nonconformance. Whenever the landlord learns of a breach of RCW 59.18.130 or has accepted performance by the tenant which is at variance with the terms of the rental agreement or rules enforceable after the commencement of the tenancy, he may immediately give notice to the tenant to remedy the nonconformance. Said notice shall expire after sixty days unless the landlord pursues any remedy under this chapter. [1973 1st ex.s. c 207 § 19.]

RCW 59.18.200   Tenancy from month to month or for rental period——Termination. When premises are rented for an indefinite time, with monthly or other periodic rent reserved, such tenancy shall be construed to be a tenancy from month to month, or from period to period on which rent is payable, and shall be terminated by written notice of twenty days or more, preceding the end of any of said months or periods, given by either party to the other. [1973 1st ex.s. c 207 § 20.]

Unlawful detainer, notice requirement: RCW 59.12.030(2).

RCW 59.18.210   Tenancies from year to year except under written contract. Tenancies from year to year are hereby abolished except when the same are created by express written contract. Leases may be in writing or print, or partly in writing and partly in print, and shall be legal and valid for any term or period not exceeding one year, without acknowledgment, witnesses or seals. [1973 1st ex.s. c 207 § 21.]

RCW 59.18.220   Termination of tenancy for a specified time. In all cases where premises are rented for a specified time, by express or implied contract, the tenancy shall be deemed terminated at the end of such specified time. [1973 1st ex.s. c 207 § 22.]

RCW 59.18.230   Waiver of chapter provisions prohibited——Provisions prohibited from rental agreement——Distress for rent abolished——Detention of personal property for rent——Remedies. (1) Any provision of a lease or other agreement, whether oral or written, whereby any section or subsection of this chapter is waived except as provided in RCW 59.18.360 and shall be deemed against public policy and shall be unenforceable. Such unenforceability shall not affect other provisions of the agreement which can be given effect without them.

(2) No rental agreement may provide that the tenant:

(a) Agrees to waive or to forego rights or remedies under this chapter; or

(b) Authorizes any person to confess judgment on a claim arising out of the rental agreement; or

(c) Agrees to pay the landlord's attorney's fees, except as authorized in this chapter; or

(d) Agrees to the exculpation or limitation of any liability of the landlord arising under law or to indemnify the landlord for that liability or the costs connected therewith; or

(e) And landlord have agreed to a particular arbitrator at the time the rental agreement is entered into.

(3) A provision prohibited by subsection (2) of this section included in a rental agreement is unenforceable. If a landlord deliberately uses a rental agreement containing provisions known by him to be prohibited, the tenant may recover actual damages sustained by him and reasonable attorney's fees.

(4) The common law right of the landlord of distress for rent is hereby abolished for property covered by this chapter. Any provision in a rental agreement creating a lien upon the personal property of the tenant or authorizing a distress for rent is null and void and of no force and effect. Any landlord who takes or detains the personal property of a tenant without the specific consent of the tenant to such incident of taking or detention, unless the property has been abandoned as described in RCW 59.18.310, and who, after written demand by the tenant for the return of his personal property, refuses or neglects to return the same promptly shall be liable to the tenant for the value of the property retained, and the prevailing party may recover his costs of suit and a reasonable attorney's fee.

In any action, including actions pursuant to chapters 7.64 or 12.28 RCW, brought by a tenant or other person to recover possession of his personal property taken or detained by a landlord in violation of this section, the court, upon motion and after notice to the opposing parties, may waive or reduce any bond requirements where it appears to be to the satisfaction of the court that the moving party is proceeding in good faith and has, prima facie, a meritorious claim for immediate delivery or redelivery of said property. [1973 1st ex.s. c 207 § 23.]

RCW 59.18.240   Reprisals or retaliatory actions by landlord——Prohibited. So long as the tenant is in compliance with this chapter, the landlord shall not take or threaten to take reprisals or retaliatory action against the tenant because of any good faith and lawful:

(1) Complaints or reports by the tenant to a governmental authority concerning the failure of the landlord to substantially comply with any code, statute, ordinance, or regulation governing the maintenance or operation of the premises, if such condition may endanger or impair the health or safety of the tenant;

(2) Assertions or enforcement by the tenant of his rights and remedies under this chapter.

"Reprisal or retaliatory action" shall mean and include but not be limited to any of the following actions by the landlord when such actions are intended primarily to retaliate against a tenant because of the tenant's good faith and lawful act:

(1) Eviction of the tenant other than giving a notice to terminate tenancy as provided in RCW 59.18.200;

(2) Increasing the rent required of the tenant;

(3) Reduction of services to the tenant;

(4) Increasing the obligations of the tenant. [1973 1st ex.s. c 207 § 24.]

RCW 59.18.250 Reprisals or retaliatory actions by landlord——Presumptions——Rebuttal——Costs. Initiation by the landlord of any action listed in RCW 59-.18.240 within ninety days after a good faith and lawful act by the tenant as enumerated in RCW 59.18.240, or within ninety days after any inspection or proceeding of a governmental agency resulting from such act, shall create a rebuttable presumption affecting the burden of proof, that the action is a reprisal or retaliatory action against the tenant: *Provided,* That if the court finds that the tenant made a complaint or report to a governmental authority within ninety days after notice of a proposed increase in rent or other action in good faith by the landlord, there is a rebuttable presumption that the complaint or report was not made in good faith: *Provided further,* That no presumption against the landlord shall arise under this section, with respect to an increase in rent, if the landlord, in a notice to the tenant of increase in rent, specifies reasonable grounds for said increase, which grounds may include a substantial increase in market value due to remedial action under this chapter: *Provided further,* That the presumption of retaliation, with respect to an eviction, may be rebutted by evidence that it is not practical to make necessary repairs while the tenant remains in occupancy. In any action or eviction proceeding where the tenant prevails upon his claim or defense that the landlord has violated this section, the tenant shall be entitled to recover his costs of suit or arbitration, including a reasonable attorney's fee, and where the landlord prevails upon his claim he shall be entitled to recover his costs of suit or arbitration, including a reasonable attorney's fee: *Provided further,* That neither party may recover attorney's fees to the extent that their legal services are provided at no cost to them. [1973 1st ex.s. c 207 § 25.]

RCW 59.18.260 Moneys paid as deposit or security for performance by tenant——Rental agreement to specify terms and conditions for retention by landlord. If any moneys are paid to the landlord by the tenant as a deposit or as security for performance of the tenant's obligations in a lease or rental agreement, such lease or rental agreement shall include the terms and conditions under which the deposit or portion thereof may be withheld by the landlord upon termination of the lease or rental agreement. If all or part of the deposit may be withheld to indemnify the landlord for damages to the premises for which the tenant is responsible, or if all or part thereof may be retained by the landlord as a nonreturnable cleaning fee, the rental agreement shall so specify. No such deposit shall be withheld on account of normal wear and tear resulting from ordinary use of the premises. [1973 1st ex.s. c 207 § 26.]

RCW 59.18.270 Moneys paid as deposit or security for performance by tenant——Deposit by landlord in trust account——Receipt——Claims. All moneys paid to the landlord by the tenant as a deposit as security for performance of the tenant's obligations in a lease or rental agreement shall promptly be deposited by the landlord in a trust account, maintained by the landlord for the purpose of holding such security deposits for tenants of the landlord, in a bank, savings and loan association, mutual savings bank, or licensed escrow agent located in Washington. Unless otherwise agreed in writing, the landlord shall be entitled to receipt of interest paid on such trust account deposits. The landlord shall provide the tenant with a written receipt for the deposit and shall provide written notice of the name and address and location of the depository and any subsequent change thereof. If during a tenancy the status of landlord is transferred to another, any sums in the deposit trust account affected by such transfer shall simultaneously be transferred to an equivalent trust account of the successor landlord, and the successor landlord shall promptly notify the tenant of the transfer and of the name, address and location of the new depository. The tenant's claim to any moneys paid under this section shall be prior to that of any creditor of the landlord, including a trustee in bankruptcy or receiver, even if such moneys are commingled. [1975 1st ex.s. c 233 § 1; 1973 1st ex.s. c 207 § 27.]

RCW 59.18.280 Moneys paid as deposit or security for performance by tenant——Statement and notice of basis for retention——Costs. Within fourteen days after the termination of the rental agreement and vacation of the premises the landlord shall give a full and specific statement of the basis for retaining any of the deposit together with the payment of any refund due the tenant under the terms and conditions of the rental agreement. No portion of any deposit shall be withheld on account of wear resulting from ordinary use of the premises.

The notice shall be delivered to the tenant personally or by mail to his last known address. If the landlord fails to give such statement together with any refund due the tenant within the time limits specified above he shall be liable to the tenant for the amount of refund due. In any action brought by the tenant to recover the deposit, the prevailing party shall additionally be entitled to the cost of suit or arbitration including a reasonable attorney's fee.

Nothing in this chapter shall preclude the landlord from proceeding against, and the landlord shall have the right to proceed against a tenant to recover sums exceeding the amount of the tenant's damage or security deposit for damage to the property for which the tenant is responsible together with reasonable attorney's fees. [1973 1st ex.s. c 207 § 28.]

RCW 59.18.290   Removal or exclusion of tenant from premises——Holding over or excluding landlord from premises after termination date. (1) It shall be unlawful for the landlord to remove or exclude from the premises the tenant thereof except under a court order so authorizing. Any tenant so removed or excluded in violation of this section may recover possession of the property or terminate the rental agreement and, in either case, may recover the actual damages sustained. The prevailing party may recover the costs of suit or arbitration and reasonable attorney's fees.

(2) It shall be unlawful for the tenant to hold over in the premises or exclude the landlord therefrom after the termination of the rental agreement except under a valid court order so authorizing. Any landlord so deprived of possession of premises in violation of this section may recover possession of the property and damages sustained by him, and the prevailing party may recover his costs of suit or arbitration and reasonable attorney's fees. [1973 1st ex.s. c 207 § 29.]

RCW 59.18.300   Termination of tenant's utility services——Tenant causing loss of landlord provided utility services. It shall be unlawful for a landlord to intentionally cause termination of any of his tenant's utility services, including water, heat, electricity, or gas, except for an interruption of utility services for a reasonable time in order to make necessary repairs. Any landlord who violates this section may be liable to such tenant for his actual damages sustained by him, and up to one hundred dollars for each day or part thereof the tenant is thereby deprived of any utility service, and the prevailing party may recover his costs of suit or arbitration and a reasonable attorney's fee. It shall be unlawful for a tenant to intentionally cause the loss of utility services provided by the landlord, including water, heat, electricity or gas, excepting as resulting from the normal occupancy of the premises. [1973 1st ex.s. c 207 § 30.]

RCW 59.18.310   Default in rent——Abandonment——Liability of tenant——Landlord's remedies. If the tenant defaults in the payment of rent and reasonably indicates by words or actions his intention not to resume tenancy, he shall be liable for the following for such abandonment: *Provided,* That upon learning of such abandonment of the premises the landlord shall make a reasonable effort to mitigate the damages resulting from such abandonment:

(1) When the tenancy is month-to-month, the tenant shall be liable for the rent for the thirty days following either the date the landlord learns of the abandonment, or the date the next regular rental payment would have become due, whichever first occurs.

(2) When the tenancy is for a term greater than month-to-month, the tenant shall be liable for the lesser of the following:

(a) The entire rent due for the remainder of the term; or

(b) All rent accrued during the period reasonably necessary to rerent the premises at a fair rental, plus the difference between such fair rental and the rent agreed to in the prior agreement, plus actual costs incurred by the landlord in rerenting the premises together with statutory court costs and reasonable attorney's fees.

In the event of such abandonment of tenancy and an accompanying default in the payment of rent by the tenant, the landlord may immediately enter and take possession of any property of the tenant found on the premises and may store the same in a secure place. A notice containing the name and address of landlord and the place where the property is stored must be mailed promptly by the landlord to the last known address of the tenant. After sixty days from the date of default in rent, and after prior notice of such sale is mailed to the last known address of the tenant, the landlord may sell such property and may apply any income derived therefrom against moneys due the landlord, including drayage and storage. Any excess income derived from the sale of such property shall be held by the landlord for the benefit of the tenant for a period of one year from the date of sale, and if no claim is made or action commenced by the tenant for the recovery thereof prior to the expiration of that period of time, the balance shall be the property of the landlord. [1973 1st ex.s. c 207 § 31.]

RCW 59.18.320   Arbitration——Authorized—— Exceptions——Notice——Procedure. (1) The landlord and tenant may agree, in writing, except as provided in RCW 59.18.230(2)(e), to submit to arbitration, in conformity with the provisions of this section, any controversy arising under the provisions of this chapter, except the following:

(a) Controversies regarding the existence of defects covered in subsections (1) and (2) of RCW 59.18.070: *Provided,* That this exception shall apply only before the implementation of any remedy by the tenant;

(b) Any situation where court action has been started by either landlord or tenant to enforce rights under this chapter; when the court action substantially affects the controversy, including but not limited to:

(i) Court action pursuant to subsections (2) and (3) of RCW 59.18.090 and subsections (1) and (2) of RCW 59.18.160; and

(ii) Any unlawful detainer action filed by the landlord pursuant to chapter 59.12 RCW.

(2) The party initiating arbitration under subsection (1) of this section shall give reasonable notice to the other party or parties.

(3) Except as otherwise provided in this section, the arbitration process shall be administered by any arbitrator agreed upon by the parties at the time the dispute arises: *Provided*, That the procedures shall comply with the requirements of chapter 7.04 RCW (relating to arbitration) and of this chapter. [1973 1st ex.s. c 207 § 32.]

RCW 59.18.330 Arbitration——Application——Hearings——Decisions. (1) Unless otherwise mutually agreed to, in the event a controversy arises under RCW 59.18.320 the landlord or tenant, or both, shall complete an application for arbitration and deliver it to the selected arbitrator.

(2) The arbitrator so designated shall schedule a hearing to be held no later than ten days following receipt of notice of the controversy, except as provided in RCW 59.18.350.

(3) The arbitrator shall conduct public or private hearings. Reasonable notice of such hearings shall be given to the parties, who shall appear and be heard either in person or by counsel or other representative. Hearings shall be informal and the rules of evidence prevailing in judicial proceedings shall not be binding. A recording of the proceedings may be taken. Any oral or documentary evidence and other data deemed relevant by the arbitrator may be received in evidence. The arbitrator shall have the power to administer oaths, to issue subpoenas, to require the attendance of witnesses and the production of such books, papers, contracts, agreements, and documents as may be deemed by the arbitrator material to a just determination of the issues in dispute. If any person refuses to obey such subpoena or refuses to be sworn to testify, or any witness, party, or attorney is guilty of any contempt while in attendance at any hearing held hereunder, the arbitrator may invoke the jurisdiction of any superior court, and such court shall have jurisdiction to issue an appropriate order. A failure to obey such order may be punished by the court as a contempt thereof.

(4) Within five days after conclusion of the hearing, the arbitrator shall make a written decision upon the issues presented, a copy of which shall be mailed by certified mail or otherwise delivered to the parties or their designated representatives. The determination of the dispute made by the arbitrator shall be final and binding upon both parties.

(5) If a defective condition exists which affects more than one dwelling unit in a similar manner, the arbitrator may consolidate the issues of fact common to those dwelling units in a single proceeding.

(6) Decisions of the arbitrator shall be enforced or appealed according to the provisions of chapter 7.04 RCW. [1973 1st ex.s. c 207 § 33.]

RCW 59.18.340 Arbitration——Fee. The administrative fee for this arbitration procedure shall be seventy dollars, and, unless otherwise allocated by the arbitrator, shall be shared equally by the parties: *Provided*, That

upon either party signing an affidavit to the effect that he is unable to pay his share of the fee, that portion of the fee may be waived or deferred. [1973 1st ex.s. c 207 § 34.]

RCW 59.18.350 Arbitration——Completion of arbitration after giving notice. When a party gives notice pursuant to subsection (2) of RCW 59.18.320, he must, at the same time, arrange for arbitration of the grievance in the manner provided in this chapter. The arbitration shall be completed before the rental due date next occurring after the giving of notice pursuant to RCW 59.18.320: *Provided*, That in no event shall the arbitrator have less than ten days to complete the arbitration process. [1973 1st ex.s. c 207 § 35.]

RCW 59.18.360 Exemptions. A landlord and tenant may agree, in writing, to exempt themselves from the provisions of RCW 59.18.060, 59.18.100, 59.18.110, 59.18.120, 59.18.130, and 59.18.190 if the following conditions have been met:

(1) The agreement may not appear in a standard form lease or rental agreement;

(2) There is no substantial inequality in the bargaining position of the two parties;

(3) The exemption does not violate the public policy of this state in favor of the ensuring safe, and sanitary housing; and

(4) Either the local county prosecutor's office or the consumer protection division of the attorney general's office or the attorney for the tenant has approved in writing the application for exemption as complying with subsections (1) through (3) of this section. [1973 1st ex.s. c 207 § 36.]

RCW 59.18.370 Forcible entry or detainer or unlawful detainer actions——Writ of restitution——Application——Order——Hearing. The plaintiff, at the time of commencing an action of forcible entry or detainer or unlawful detainer, or at any time afterwards, upon filing the complaint, may apply to the superior court in which the action is pending for an order directing the defendant to appear and show cause, if any he has, why a writ of restitution should not issue restoring to the plaintiff possession of the property in the complaint described, and the judge shall by order fix a time and place for a hearing of said motion, which shall not be less than six nor more than twelve days from the date of service of said order upon defendant. A copy of said order, together with a copy of the summons and complaint if not previously served upon the defendant, shall be served upon the defendant. Said order shall notify the defendant that if he fails to appear and show cause at the time and place specified by the order the court may order the sheriff to restore possession of the property to the plaintiff and may grant such other relief as may be prayed for in the complaint and provided by this chapter. [1973 1st ex.s. c 207 § 38.]

RCW 59.18.380 Forcible entry or detainer or unlawful detainer actions——Writ of restitution——Answer——Order——Stay——Bond. At the time and place fixed for the hearing of plaintiff's motion for a writ of restitution, the defendant, or any person in possession or claiming possession of the property, may answer, orally or in writing, and assert any legal or equitable defense or set-off arising out of the tenancy. If the answer is oral the substance thereof shall be endorsed on the complaint by the court. The court shall examine the parties and witnesses orally to ascertain the merits of the complaint and answer, and if it shall appear that the plaintiff has the right to be restored to possession of the property, the court shall enter an order directing the issuance of a writ of restitution, returnable ten days after its date, restoring to the plaintiff possession of the property and if it shall appear to the court that there is no substantial issue of material fact of the right of the plaintiff to be granted other relief as prayed for in the complaint and provided for in this chapter, the court may enter an order and judgment granting so much of such relief as may be sustained by the proof, and the court may grant such other relief as may be prayed for in the plaintiff's complaint and provided for in this chapter, then the court shall enter an order denying any relief sought by the plaintiff for which the court has determined that the plaintiff has no right as a matter of law: Provided, That within three days after the service of the writ of restitution the defendant, or person in possession of the property, may, in any action for the recovery of possession of the property for failure to pay rent, stay the execution of the writ pending final judgment by paying into court or to the plaintiff, as the court directs, all rent found to be due and all the costs of the action, and in addition by paying, on a monthly basis pending final judgment, an amount equal to the monthly rent called for by the lease or rental agreement at the time the complaint was filed: Provided further, That before any writ shall issue prior to final judgment the plaintiff shall execute to the defendant and file in the court a bond in such sum as the court may order, with sufficient surety to be approved by the clerk, conditioned that the plaintiff will prosecute his action without delay, and will pay all costs that may be adjudged to the defendant, and all damages which he may sustain by reason of the writ of restitution having been issued, should the same be wrongfully sued out. The court shall also enter an order directing the parties to proceed to trial on the complaint and answer in the usual manner.

If it appears to the court that the plaintiff should not be restored to possession of the property, the court shall deny plaintiff's motion for a writ of restitution and enter an order directing the parties to proceed to trial within thirty days on the complaint and answer. If it appears to the court that there is a substantial issue of material fact as to whether or not the plaintiff is entitled to other relief as is prayed for in plaintiff's complaint and provided for in this chapter, or that there is a genuine issue of a material fact pertaining to a legal or equitable defense or set-off raised in the defendant's answer, the court shall grant or deny so much of plaintiff's other relief

sought and so much of defendant's defenses or set-off claimed, as may be proper. [1973 1st ex.s. c 207 § 39.]

RCW 59.18.390 Forcible entry or detainer or unlawful detainer actions——Writ of restitution——Service——Defendant's bond. The sheriff shall, upon receiving the writ of restitution, forthwith serve a copy thereof upon the defendant, his agent, or attorney, or a person in possession of the premises, and shall not execute the same for three days thereafter, and the defendant, or person in possession of the premises within three days after the service of the writ of restitution may execute to the plaintiff a bond to be filed with and approved by the clerk of the court in such sum as may be fixed by the judge, with sufficient surety to be approved by the clerk of said court, conditioned that they will pay to the plaintiff such sum as the plaintiff may recover for the use and occupation of the said premises, or any rent found due, together with all damages the plaintiff may sustain by reason of the defendant occupying or keeping possession of said premises, together with all damages which the court theretofore has awarded to the plaintiff as provided in this chapter, and also all the costs of the action. The plaintiff, his agent or attorneys, shall have notice of the time and place where the court or judge thereof shall fix the amount of the defendant's bond, and shall have notice and a reasonable opportunity to examine into the qualification and sufficiency of the sureties upon said bond before said bond shall be approved by the clerk. The writ may be served by the sheriff, in the event he shall be unable to find the defendant, an agent or attorney, or a person in possession of the premises, by affixing a copy of said writ in a conspicuous place upon the premises. [1973 1st ex.s. c 207 § 40.]

RCW 59.18.400 Forcible entry or detainer or unlawful detainer actions——Writ of restitution——Answer of defendant. On or before the day fixed for his appearance the defendant may appear and answer. The defendant in his answer may assert any legal or equitable defense or set-off arising out of the tenancy. [1973 1st ex.s. c 207 § 41.]

RCW 59.18.410 Forcible entry or detainer or unlawful detainer actions——Writ of restitution——Judgment——Execution. If upon the trial the verdict of the jury or, if the case be tried without a jury, the finding of the court be in favor of the plaintiff and against the defendant, judgment shall be entered for the restitution of the premises; and if the proceeding be for unlawful detainer after neglect or failure to perform any condition or covenant of a lease or agreement under which the property is held, or after default in the payment of rent, the judgment shall also declare the forfeiture of the lease, agreement or tenancy. The jury, or the court, if the proceedings be tried without a jury, shall also assess the damages arising out of the tenancy occasioned to the plaintiff by any forcible entry, or by any forcible or unlawful detainer, alleged in the complaint and proved on the trial, and, if the alleged unlawful detainer be after default in the payment of rent, find the amount of any rent due, and the judgment shall be rendered against the defendant guilty of the forcible entry, forcible detainer or unlawful detainer for the amount of damages thus assessed and for the rent, if any, found due, and the court may award statutory costs and reasonable attorney's fees. When the proceeding is for an unlawful detainer after default in the payment of rent, and the lease or agreement under which the rent is payable has not by its terms expired, execution upon the judgment shall not be issued until the expiration of five days after the entry of the judgment, within which time the tenant or any subtenant, or any mortgagee of the term, or other party interested in the continuance of the tenancy, may pay into court for the landlord the amount of the judgment and costs, and thereupon the judgment shall be satisfied and the tenant restored to his tenancy; but if payment, as herein provided, be not made within five days the judgment may be enforced for its full amount and for the possession of the premises. In all other cases the judgment may be enforced immediately. If writ of restitution shall have been executed prior to judgment no further writ or execution for the premises shall be required. [1973 1st ex.s. c 207 § 42.]

RCW 59.18.415 Applicability to certain single family dwelling leases. The provisions of this chapter shall not apply to any lease of a single family dwelling for a period of a year or more or to any lease of a single family dwelling containing a bona fide purchase by the tenant: *Provided,* That attorney for the tenant must approve on the face of the agreement any lease exempted from the provisions of this chapter as provided for in this section. [1973 1st ex.s. c 207 § 43.]

RCW 59.18.420 RCW 59.12.090, 59.12.100, 59.12-.121 and 59.12.170 inapplicable. The provisions of RCW 59.12.090, 59.12.100, 59.12.121, and 59.12.170 shall not apply to any rental agreement included under the provisions of chapter 59.18 RCW. [1973 1st ex.s. c 207 § 44.]

RCW 59.18.430 Applicability to prior, existing or future leases. RCW 59.18.010 through 59.18.360 and 59.18.900 shall not apply to any lease entered into prior to July 16, 1973. All provisions of this chapter shall apply to any lease or periodic tenancy entered into on or subsequent to July 16, 1973. [1973 1st ex.s. c 207 § 47.]

RCW 59.18.900 Severability——1973 1st ex.s. c 207. If any provision of this chapter, or its application to any person or circumstance is held invalid, the remainder of the act, or its application to other persons or circumstances, is not affected. [1973 1st ex.s. c 207 § 37.]

Appendix B

Sample Forms

TO: _____ B. TENANT _____
                                        (Name of Tenant)
Tenant(s) in possession of ____H____
                          (Apartment No.)

____Baltic Street Apartments_____
                                        (Name of Building)

____718 Baltic Street_____   Seattle_____
(Street Address)   (City)

__King__ County, Washington, at a monthly rental of __$90.00____

   You are hereby notified that you are delinquent in the payment of rent
for the above described premises in the sum of $ __90.00__ for the
period from __Oct. 1__, 19__77__, to __Oct. 31__, 19__77__.

   You are hereby required to pay said rent in the full sum of $ __90.00__
or in the alternative, to surrender said premises to the undersigned
owner, or his agents set forth below, within three (3) days after the
service of this notice upon you.

   In the event of your failure to do so within the said period, you will be
guilty of unlawful detainer and subject to eviction as provided by law.

   Dated at __Seattle__, Washington, this __15th__ day of __October__,
19__77__.

                        Apartments__BALTIC STREET APARTMENTS__

                            Owner__J. LANDLORD_____

                              By__R. JONES_____
                                                (Agent)

1. *Three-day notice to pay rent or vacate*

TO: ____B. TENANT_____
                                    (Name of Tenant)

Tenant(s) in possession of ____H____
                          (Apartment No.)

_Baltic Street Apartments_____
                                    (Name of Building)

_718 Baltic Street_____   Seattle____
(Street Address)   (City)

_King___ County, Washington.

You are hereby notified that you have failed to perform the following condition(s) or covenant(s) in your rental agreement:

_____You have two dogs in your apartment_____

_____in violation of the no-pets rule contained_

_____in Paragraph 18 of your rental agreement.__

You are required to comply with ____the no-pets rule___

_contained in Paragraph 18 of your rental_____

_agreement_____
or in the alternative to surrender said premises to the undersigned owner, or his agents set forth below, within (10) days after service of this notice upon you.

In the event of your failure to do so within the said period, you will be guilty of unlawful detainer and subject to eviction as provided by law.

Dated at _Seattle_, Washington, this __10th__ day of _October_, 19_77_.

Apartments_BALTIC STREET APARTMENTS__

Owner____J. LANDLORD_____

By____R. JONES_____
                            (Agent)

2. *Ten-day notice to perform covenant of rental agreement or vacate*

TO: _____ B. TENANT _____

YOU ARE HEREBY NOTIFIED AND REQUIRED TO REMOVE FROM
AND DELIVER UP TO THE UNDERSIGNED POSSESSION OF THE
PREMISES NOW HELD AND OCCUPIED BY YOU BEING THOSE
CERTAIN PREMISES SITUATED IN THE CITY OF __Seattle__,
__King__ COUNTY, WASHINGTON AND PARTICULARLY DE-
SCRIBED AS FOLLOWS:

__Apt. H__   Baltic Street Apartments
(Apartment Number)   (Name of Building)

__718 Baltic Street__   Seattle , WASHINGTON
(Street Address)   (City)

WITHIN THREE (3) DAYS AFTER THE SERVICE OF THIS NOTICE
UPON YOU, OR THE UNDERSIGNED WILL INSTITUTE LEGAL PRO-
CEEDINGS AGAINST YOU TO RECOVER POSSESSION OF SAID
PREMISES. THIS NOTICE IS SERVED UPON YOU ON THE GROUND
AND FOR THE REASON THAT YOU HAVE COMMITTED AND ARE
COMMITTING A NUISANCE AND WASTE UPON THE PREMISES.

DATED AT __Seattle__, WASHINGTON, THIS __10th__ DAY OF
__October__, 19__77__.

THIS NOTICE IS GIVEN YOU PURSUANT TO THE PROVISIONS OF
SECTION 59.12.030(5) OF THE REVISED CODE OF WASHINGTON.

_____ J. LANDLORD _____
                                (Owner)

_____ R. JONES _____
                                (Agent)

3. *Three-day notice to quit premises*

TO: _____B. TENANT_____ tenant(s) in possession:

You are hereby notified that your tenancy of the apartment described below is herewith terminated effective on the ___31st___ day of October, 19 77.

You are hereby notified and required to remove from and deliver up to the undersigned owner, possession of the premises now held and occupied by you, being those certain premises situated in the City of Seattle, County of __King__, State of Washington, and more particularly described as follows:

_____H_____	Baltic Street Apartments
(Apartment Number)	(Name of Building)

_718 Baltic Street_____	Seattle__, WASHINGTON
(Street Address)	(City)

Dated at _Seattle_ Washington, this ___5th___ day of October, 19 77.

This notice is given pursuant to the provisions of the Washington Residential Landlord-Tenant Act, RCW 59.18.200.

Apartments BALTIC STREET APARTMENTS

Owner____J. LANDLORD_____

By___R. JONES_____

(Agent)

4. *Notice to terminate tenancy*

IN THE SUPERIOR COURT OF THE STATE OF WASHINGTON FOR KING COUNTY

J. LANDLORD,	)	
Plaintiff,	)	NO. 8 0 4 3 3 9
	)	
v.	)	SUMMONS
	)	
B. TENANT,	)	
	)	
Defendant.	)	

THE STATE OF WASHINGTON TO: B. Tenant, Defendant

      YOU ARE HEREBY SUMMONED AND DIRECTED to appear and answer the complaint in the above entitled action on or before the 20th day of April, 1977, on which day this summons is made returnable, and to serve a copy of your answer upon the under-signed attorney for the plaintiff at the office below stated, and in case of your failure to do so, judgment will be taken against you for the relief sought as hereinafter set forth, and as likewise particularly set forth in the complaint, which complaint is filed with the clerk of said court, and a copy of which is herewith served upon you.

      YOU ARE FURTHER NOTIFIED that this is an action for unlawful detainer and that the relief sought in this action is to recover possession of the premises hereinafter described, for judgment for the amount of rent found due and damages that have been and will be occasioned to the plaintiff by and during your unlawful detention of said premises, which premises are situated in the city of Seattle, county of King, state of Washington, and are particularly described as follows:

                Apartment H at 718 Baltic Street,
                Seattle, Washington

      DATED this 8th day of April, 1977.

                PEFFER, SNAGSBY & PARDIGGLE

                By_____
                  MILTON SNAGSBY
                  Attorney for Plaintiff

                Law Offices of:

SUMMONS   PEFFER, SNAGSBY & PARDIGGLE
                          6004 National Bank Building
                          Seattle, Washington 98154
                          800-1204

5. Summons

IN THE SUPERIOR COURT OF THE STATE OF WASHINGTON FOR KING COUNTY

J. LANDLORD,)
)
       Plaintiff,)   NO. 8 0 4 3 3 9
)
       v   )   COMPLAINT FOR
)   UNLAWFUL DETAINER
B. TENANT,)
)
       Defendant.)

      Plaintiff alleges as follows:

                        I.

      That plaintiff, as landlord, rented to defendant, as tenant, the premises consisting of an apartment commonly known as Apartment H, Baltic Street Apartments, 718 Baltic Street, in the City of Seattle, County of King, State of Washington, to be held and possessed by the defendant on a month-to-month tenancy under which the rent due from the defendant to plaintiff was and is ninety dollars ($90.00) per month payable in advance on the first day of each calendar month, and that the defendant has been and is now in actual possession and occupation of said premises.

                        II.

      That on the 5th day of March, 1977, the plaintiff caused to be served upon defendant a notice of termination of tenancy, whereby the defendant's tenancy at said premises was terminated as of March 31, 1977. A true copy of the notice of termination is attached.

                       III.

      That notwithstanding the notice of termination, the defendant has continued in possession of the premises and is now in the unlawful possession thereof.

                     Law Offices of:

COMPLAINT   PEFFER, SNAGSBY & PARDIGGLE
                        6004 National Bank Building
                        Seattle, Washington   98154
                        800-1204

6. *Complaint for unlawful detainer*

IV.

That the reasonable rental value of said premises is $90.00 per month, or $3.00 per day.

V.

That a reasonable sum to be allowed to plaintiff's counsel for his services herein is the sum of $200.00, if this action is not contested, and such further sums as the court may deem reasonable in the event of contest.

WHEREFORE, plaintiff prays for judgment against the defendant, B. Tenant, as follows:

1. For restitution of the above described premises;

2. For forfeiture and termination of the defendant's tenancy;

3. For judgment against the defendant in the sum of $3.00 for each day he continues to occupy said premises on and after March 31, 1977, until he vacates said premises.

4. For plaintiff's cost of suit and reasonable attorney's fees in the sum of $200.00 if this action is not contested and such further sums as the court may deem reasonable in the event of contest; and

5. For such other and further relief as the court may deem just and proper.

Dated this 8th day of April, 1977.

PEFFER, SNAGSBY & PARDIGGLE

By: _____
    MILTON SNAGSBY
    Attorney for Plaintiff

COMPLAINT - 2

IN THE SUPERIOR COURT OF THE STATE OF WASHINGTON FOR KING COUNTY

J. LANDLORD,	)	
Plaintiff,	)	NO. 8 0 4 3 3 9
	)	ORDER TO SHOW CAUSE
v.	)	
	)	
B. TENANT,	)	
	)	
Defendant.	)	

THIS MATTER having come on for hearing before the above entitled court and the court having read and considered the plaintiff's motion for an order to show cause why a writ of restitution should not be issued restoring to the plaintiff the possession of the premises described in the complaint and it appearing that there is sufficient cause for the issuance of such order, now, therefore, it is hereby

ORDERED, that the defendant, B. Tenant, be and he is hereby required to appear in Room W-623 of the King County Court-house in Seattle, Washington at the hour of 9:30 a.m. on the 20th day of April, 1977, or as soon thereafter as the matter may be heard, then and there to show cause, if any he may have, why the court should not order the Sheriff to restore possession to the plaintiff of the premises the defendant is occupying and holding as tenant of plaintiff of the premises at 718 Baltic Street, Apartment H, Seattle, King County, Washington.

DONE IN OPEN COURT this 8th day of April, 1977.

_____
J U D G E/ COURT COMMISSIONER

Presented by:

_____
PEFFER, SNAGSBY & PARDIGGLE
Attorneys for Plaintiff

ORDER TO SHOW CAUSE

Law Offices of:

PEFFER, SNAGSBY & PARDIGGLE
6004 National Bank Building
Seattle, Washington   98154
800-1204

7. *Order to show cause*

IN THE SUPERIOR COURT OF THE STATE OF WASHINGTON FOR KING COUNTY

J. LANDLORD,

              Plaintiff,

        v.

B. TENANT,

              Defendant.

NO. 8 0 4 3 3 9

ANSWER, AFFIRMATIVE
DEFENSES, SET-OFFS

The defendant answers plaintiff's complaint as follows:

1. Admits the allegations contained in paragraphs one and two.

2. Admits that portion of paragraph three alleging that defendant has continued in possession of the premises but denies that such possession is unlawful.

3. Denies the allegations contained in paragraphs four and five.

Affirmative Defenses and Set-offs

As affirmative defenses and set-offs, defendant alleges as follows:

4. Plaintiff failed to serve a twenty-day notice of termination of tenancy on defendant in the manner required by RCW 59.12.040 thus depriving this court of jurisdiction.

5. Plaintiff has allowed substantial defects to exist on the premises during the entire term of defendant's tenancy. These defects include but are not limited to the following:

    a. Broken windows;

    b. Rotted window frames which make it impossible to open the windows or lock them;

    c. Holes in the floors, walls, and ceiling;

ANSWER, AFFIRMATIVE
DEFENSES, SET-OFFS

RACHEL ROE
20th Floor, Bank Building
Seattle, Washington 98101
802-4589

8. Answer, affirmative defenses, set-offs

d. A total absence of heat and leaking gas from gas stove;

e. Broken and defective plumbing.

6. Plaintiff has been given notice of these defects several times: actual notice upon entering the premises; verbal notice from the defendant; several written notices from the building department of code violations; and a written notice from the defendant sent on January 1, 1977.

7. In spite of these notices, plaintiff has failed and/or refused to make the needed repairs and maintain the premises in a condition fit for human habitation.

8. Plaintiff's failure and/or refusal to remedy the conditions set forth in paragraph 5 above, during the entire term of the tenancy of defendant, constitutes a breach of the implied warranty of habitability, relieving defendant of his obligation to pay rent.

9. The actions of plaintiff constitute a breach of his obligations under the Housing Code, Seattle Ordinance No. 99112, enacted on August 30, 1970 and Seattle Ordinance No. 106319, enacted on April 24, 1977, requiring that all buildings be maintained at minimum building code standards.

10. Plaintiff's attempt to terminate defendant's tenancy is solely in retaliation for his good faith and lawful assertion of his rights and remedies under the Residential Landlord-Tenant Act, RCW 59.18.010 et seq.

11. Plaintiff has breached the implied warranty of habitability, and defendant suffered damage as a result of the reduced value of his property.

12. Defendant is entitled to a set-off against any damages found to be due and owing in the form of a retroactive abatement of his rent based upon the difference between the agreed rental value of his apartment and the actual value of his

ANSWER, AFFIRMATIVE
DEFENSES, SET-OFFS - 2

apartment in its deteriorated and delapidated condition.

WHEREFORE, defendant requests the following relief:

1. That plaintiff's complaint be dismissed with pre-judice and defendant be awarded his costs, disbursements, and reasonable attorney's fees.

2. That defendant be awarded a retroactive rebate of all rent paid to plaintiff during the entire term of defendant's tenancy, in the amount of 85 percent.

Dated this 19th day of April, 1977.

RACHEL ROE
Attorney for Defendant

ANSWER, AFFIRMATIVE
DEFENSES, SET-OFFS - 3

In the Superior Court of the State of Washington

for the County of King

J. LANDLORD,

_____

_____

                       Plaintiff

        vs.

B. TENANT,

_____

_____

                       Defendant

No. 8 0 4 3 3 9

WRIT OF RESTITUTION

STATE OF WASHINGTON,
To the SHERIFF OF KING COUNTY, *Greeting*:

WHEREAS, on the ....20th.... day of ....April............ , 19 77 , on motion of the Attorney.... for the plaintiff.... in the above entitled action, Honorable ....James Jones.... one of the Judges of the above entitled Court made an order granting a writ of Restitution restoring possession of the premises described in the Plaintiff's complaint filed herein in the manner provided by law.

NOW, THEREFORE, You the said Sheriff, are hereby commanded to deliver to the said Plaintiff, the possession of the premises described in said complaint, to wit:

Apartment H – Baltic Street Apartments,

718 Baltic Street, Seattle, Washington

in the County of ....King...... , State of Washington, and make return of this writ according to law.

WITNESS the Hon. ....James Jones.................... , Judge of the said Superior Court, and seal thereof, this ..20th.... day of ....April............ , 19 77 .

(SEAL)

BETTY J. MULLEN, Superior Court Clerk

By ...... W. L. PROCTOR ......

                                          Deputy.

9. Writ of restitution

IN THE SEATTLE DISTRICT COURT
KING COUNTY, STATE OF WASHINGTON

B. TENANT
Plaintiff (name)

718 Baltic Street,   338-4167
Address - phone number

J. LANDLORD
Defendant (name)

1434 Park Place,   424-9083
Address - phone number

NOTICE OF SMALL CLAIM

NO. ___6281___

In the name of the STATE OF WASHINGTON you, the above named defendant, are directed to appear personally and answer the claim of the above named plaintiff, at Seattle District Justice Court, Room 327, King County Court House, Seattle, Washington on

November 2, 1977

at ___9:30 a.m.___ , ready for trial, and to have available all records and evidence necessary to establish a defense to the claim.

You are further notified that in case you do not appear judgement will be rendered against you in the amount of the claim as stated, plus court costs.

10/8/77
Date Issued   SMALL CLAIM

/s/ Clerk
Clerk, Seattle District Court

The plaintiff alleges that on the __15th__ day of _____September_____ , 19_77_ ,

the defendant became indebted to the plaintiff in the sum of $ _____50.00_____

for ___failure to return damage deposit___
(Auto damages, wages, rent loan, goods, etc.)

and that although plaintiff has made demand upon the defendant, the defendant refuses to pay the same.

The plaintiff prays for judgement against the defendant as alleges above, plus court costs.

STATE OF WASHINGTON)
) ss
COUNTY OF KING   )

B. TENANT

The undersigned, being first duly sworn, deposes and says, I am the plaintiff above named.

I have read the foregoing claim, know the contents thereof, and believe the same to be true.

B. TENANT
Plaintiff

Subscribed and sworn to before me this ___8th___ day of ___October, 1977.___

/s/ Clerk
Clerk, Seattle District Court

10. *Notice of small claim*

SEATTLE DISTRICT COURT, KING COUNTY, STATE OF WASHINGTON

SMALL CLAIMS COURT

B. TENANT,	)
Plaintiff,	) NO. 6 2 8 1
v.	) AFFIDAVIT OF
J. LANDLORD,	) SERVICE
Defendant.	)

STATE OF WASHINGTON)
) ss.
COUNTY OF KING   )

      R. Doe, being first duly sworn, upon oath deposes and says:

      At all times herein mentioned, I was and am now a citizen of the United States, a resident of the State of Washington, over the age of eighteen years and competent to be a witness in this action.

      On the 26th day of October, 1977, at 7:30 a.m., at 1434 Park Place, Seattle, King County, Washington, I served the Notice of Small Claim in this action upon the defendant J. LANDLORD, by then and there delivering to and leaving personally with him a full, true, and correct copy of the Notice of Small Claim.

                        /s/ R. DOE

      SUBSCRIBED and SWORN to before me this 29th day of October, 1977.

                        /s/ A. SMITH
                        NOTARY PUBLIC in and for
                        the State of Washington,
                        residing at Seattle.

11. Affidavit of service

IN THE SEATTLE DISTRICT COURT

KING COUNTY, STATE OF WASHINGTON

SMALL CLAIMS COURT

COUNTERCLAIM

NO. __6281__

To Plaintiff ____B. TENANT_____

The Defendant herein alleges that the Plaintiff is indebted to the Defendant

in the sum of $ __100.00_____ for __property damage to premises__

__located at 718 Baltic Street, Apt. H, Seattle, Washington 98144.__

_____

on __August 31, 1977._____ and that the Defendant has made demand upon

the Plaintiff and that Plaintiff refuses to pay same.

WHEREFORE, the Defendant prays that Plainriff's case be dismissed and prays

for judgment as alleged above, plus court costs.

STATE OF WASHINGTON)
) ss
COUNTY OF KING   )   __Sig/s/   J. LANDLORD_____
                                            Defendant

The undersigned, being duly sworn, deposes and says, I am the Defendant

herein, I have read the foregoing claim, know the contents thereof, and

believe the same to be true.

                                    __Sig/s/   J. LANDLORD_____
                                            Defendant

Subscribed and sworn to before me this __27th__ day of ___October, 1977.___

                                __/s/ Clerk_____
                                Clerk, Seattle District Court

12. Counterclaim

Appendix C

Legal Services Offices in Washington by County

Asotin/Whitman:
Evergreen Legal Services
Asotin/Whitman Office
836½ Sixth Street
Clarkston, Washington 99403
(509) 758-1618

Benton/Franklin:
Evergreen Legal Services
Benton/Franklin Office
200 South Wehe
Matrix Bldg. — Suite 3
Pasco, Washington 99301
(509) 547-8370

Clallam/Jefferson:
Evergreen Legal Services
Clallam/Jefferson Office
805 East Eighth Street
Port Angeles, Washington 98362
(206) 452-3368

Ferry/Stevens/Pend O:
Spokane Legal Services
Tri-County Office
219 South Elm
Colville, Washington 99114
(509) 684-5282

Grant/Adams:
Evergreen Legal Services
Grant/Adams Office
224 West Broadway
Moses Lake, Washington 98837
(509) 765-9221

King:
Evergreen Legal Services
Seattle Central Area Office
1411 21st Avenue
Seattle, Washington 98122
(206) 464-5941

and

Seattle Pioneer Square Office
618 Second Avenue
Seattle, Washington 98104
(206) 464-5911

Kitsap:
Evergreen Legal Services
Kitsap Office
Room 215
Medical-Dental Bldg.
Bremerton, Washington 98310
(206) 377-7694

Kittitas/Chelan:
Evergreen Legal Services
Kittitas/Chelan Office
306 North Main
Ellensburg, Washington 98926
(509) 925-5354

Pierce:
Puget Sound Legal Assistance
744 Market Street
Tacoma, Washington 98402
(206) 572-4343

Skagit/Island:
Evergreen Legal Services
Skagit/Island Office
112 Broadway
Mt. Vernon, Washington 98273
(206) 336-5784

Snohomish:
Evergreen Legal Services
Snohomish Office
1712½ Hewitt Avenue
Everett, Washington 98201
(206) 258-2681

Spokane:
Spokane Legal Services
West 246 Riverside Avenue
Spokane, Washington 99201
(509) 838-3671

Thurston/Mason:
Puget Sound Legal
Assistance Foundation
529 West Fourth
Olympia, Washington 98501
(206) 943-6260

Walla Walla/Columbia/Garfield:
Evergreen Legal Services
Walla Walla/Columbia/Garfield Office
13½ East Main
Walla Walla, Washington 99362
(509) 529-7070

Whatcom/San Juan:
Evergreen Legal Services
Whatcom/San Juan Office
203 West Holly, Room 32
Bellingham, Washington 98225
(206) 734-8680

Yakima:
Evergreen Legal Services
Yakima Office
6 East "A" Street
Yakima, Washington 98901
(509) 453-8951

and

Evergreen Legal Services
Sunnyside Office
501 East Edison
Sunnyside, Washington 98944
(509) 837-4520

Notes

Chapter 1

1. When Governor Evans signed the Landlord-Tenant Act in 1973 he vetoed fourteen provisions that he thought were unfair to tenants. In May 1977 the Supreme Court ruled that those vetoes were improper. The effect of the court's decision was to put those vetoed sections back in the Act. *Washington Association of Apartment Associations, Inc. v. Daniel J. Evans*, 88 Wn.2d 563, 564 P.2d 788 (1977).

2. To determine whether a tenant is covered by the Landlord-Tenant Act it is necessary to look at both RCW 59.18.030 and RCW 59.18.040.

3. The Washington State Legislature has adopted a law to cover mobile home landlord-tenant relations, which went into effect September 21, 1977. SB 2324.

4. It is unclear whether this exclusion requires the approval of the tenant's attorney. RCW 59.18.415.

5. RCW 59.18.415.

6. RCW 59.12.170. Double damages may be subject to a constitutional challenge. See *Lindsey v. Normet*, 405 U.S. 56, 92 S. Ct. 862, 31 L. Ed.2d 36 (1972).

7. RCW 59.18.420.

8. RCW 59.12.090. This pre-trial writ of restitution may be subject to a constitutional challenge. See *North Georgia Finishing v. Di-Chem*, 419 U.S. 601, 95 S. Ct. 719, 42 L. Ed.2d 751 (1975).

9. RCW 59.18.370 and .380.

10. RCW 4.84.080 and RCW 12.20.060.

11. RCW 59.18.030 (9).

Chapter 2

1. For a general discussion of types of tenancies see Stoebuck, *The Law between Landlord and Tenant in Washington: Part I*, 49 WASH. L. REV. 291, 312–31 (1974). Two less common types of tenancies are:

(a) Tenancy at Will—where both parties are free to terminate the tenancy at any time without advance notice. The landlord, however, must give a tenant a reasonable period of time to move out. Tenants who are employed by their landlord and live on the premises may be tenants at will. See *Najewitz v. City of Seattle*, 21 Wn.2d 656, 152 P.2d 722 (1944).

(b) Tenancy at Sufferance—where a trespasser moves in without permission of the landlord. RCW 59.04.050.

2. RCW 59.18.200.

3. RCW 59.04.030.

4. *Armstrong v. Burkett*, 104 Wash. 476, 177 P. 333 (1918).

5. In the Landlord-Tenant Act the term "rental agreement" is used to refer to both leases and month-to-month agreements. RCW 59.18.030 (6).

6. *H. D. Fowler Co. v. Warren*, 17 Wn. App. 178, 562 P.2d 649 (1977). Illegal rental agreement provisions are contained in RCW 59.18.230.

7. *Hopkins v. Barlin*, 31 Wn.2d 260, 196 P.2d 347 (1948); *Rockwell v. Eiler's Music House*, 67 Wash. 478, 122 P. 12 (1912). This rule of law is called the "parol evidence" rule.

8. RCW 59.18.230.

9. RCW 59.18.230 (3).

10. These sections are RCW 59.18.060, RCW 59.18.100, RCW 59.18.110, RCW 59.18.120, RCW 59.18.130, and RCW 59.18.190.

11. RCW 59.18.360 specifies how a landlord and tenant may waive these sections of the Landlord-Tenant Act.

Chapter 3

1. RCW 59.18.060.

2. RCW 59.18.230 (2) (a).

3. Seattle, Washington, Ordinance 106319, April 24, 1977. Seattle's minimum housing code applies to all existing rental housing. It is known and cited as the "Housing Code."

4. RCW 59.18.060 (11); RCW 59.18.130 (4).

Chapter 4

1. RCW 59.18.130.

2. Additional duties may be imposed by local housing or health codes. The Seattle Housing Code, for example, has a specific section on duties of tenants. Seattle Ordinance 106319,chapter 4, section 4.16. (April 24, 1977).

3. See chapter 10, pp. 61–62 for an explanation of what is considered a nuisance or waste.

4. RCW 59.18.160.

5. RCW 59.18.180.

6. *Bernard v. Triangle Music Co.*, 1 Wn.2d 41, 95 P.2d 43 (1939).

7. RCW 59.18.140.

8. 42 U.S.C. §1437 (a).

9. RCW 59.18.240.

10. RCW 59.18.140.

11. *Ferguson v. Hoshi*, 25 Wash. 664, 66 P. 105 (1901).

12. The Act imposes a general obligation of good faith. RCW 59.18.020. Tenants cannot be forced to waive rights under the Act. RCW 59.18.230.

13. RCW 59.18.140.

14. *Blakely v. Housing Authority*, 8 Wn. App. 204, 505 P.2d 151 (1973).

15. RCW 59.18.230; RCW 49.60.222.

16. RCW 59.18.240.

Chapter 5

1. RCW 59.18.080.

2. RCW 59.18.070.

3. RCW 59.18.060 (11).

4. RCW 59.18.070 (4).

5. RCW 59.18.100 (3).

6. Labor costs are computed by looking at the prevailing rate in the community for performing the same type of work. RCW 59.18.100 (3).

7. RCW 59.18.100 (1).

8. RCW 59.18.100; the self-help repair procedure and the bid repair procedure are contained in two different subsections. You are entitled to the maximum rent reduction under each subsection.

9. RCW 59.18.090.

10. RCW 59.18.110.

11. *Foisy v. Wyman*, 83 Wn.2d 22, 515 P.2d 160 (1973). The facts in *Foisy* occurred before the passage of the Residential Landlord-Tenant Act of 1973 and the Act did not apply.

12. *Berzito v. Gambino*, 63 N.J. 460, 308 A.2d 17 (1973); *Foisy v. Wyman*, 83 Wn.2d 22, 515 P.2d 160 (1973).

13. RCW 59.18.080.

14. RCW 59.18.320.

15. RCW 59.18.230 (2) (e).

16. RCW 59.18.320; RCW 7.04.

17. RCW 59.18.090 (1).

18. *Foisy v. Wyman*, see note 11.

Chapter 6

1. Members of your family or guests may also be able to recover damages for injuries. See Stoebuck, *The Law between Landlord and Tenant in Washington: Part I*, 49 WASH. L. REV. 291, 352 (1974).

2. It has been suggested that a landlord may be held liable for injuries caused by a defect on the premises regardless of whether he knew or should have known about the defect. This theory of liability is known as "strict liability." See *Kaplan v. Coulston*, 381 N.Y.S.2d 634 (1976); *Golden v. Conway*, 55 Cal. App. 3d 948, 128 Cal. Rptr. 69 (1976).

3. See *Thomas v. Housing Auth. of Bremerton*, 71 Wn.2d 69, 426 P.2d 836 (1967); *Geise v. Lee*, 84 Wn.2d 866, 529 P.2d 1054 (1975).

4. See *Braitman v. Overlook Terrace Corp.*, 68 N.J. 368, 346 A.2d 76 (1975); *Kline v. 1500 Mass. Ave. Apt. Corp.*, 439 F.2d 477 (D.C. Cir. 1970).

5. RCW 59.18.230 (2) (d); *McCutcheon v. United Homes Corp.*, 79 Wn.2d 443, 486 P.2d 1093 (1971).

6. The measure of damages for personal injuries is discussed in *Dyal v. Fire Cos. Adjustment Bureau*, 23 Wn.2d 515, 161 P.2d 321 (1945).

Chapter 7

1. RCW 59.18.150.

2. RCW 59.18.230 (2) (a).

3. RCW 59.18.110.

4. The criminal trespass statute is RCW 9.83.080; first and second degree burglary are defined in RCW 9.19.010 and RCW 9.19.020. A general discussion of the possibility of criminal prosecution of landlords for unlawful entry is contained in a Washington State Attorney General Opinion dated May 16, 1974, which is cited as AGO 1974 No. 10.

5. *Haase v. Helgeson*, 57 Wn.2d 863, 360 P.2d 339 (1961).

Chapter 8

1. RCW 59.18.200.
2. RCW 59.18.310.
3. See Stoebuck, *The Law between Landlord and Tenant in Washington: Part II*, 49 WASH. L. REV. 1013, 1085 (1974).
4. RCW 59.18.310.
5. *Tuschoff v. Westover*, 65 Wn.2d 69, 395 P.2d 630 (1964). An intention not to occupy the place is not necessarily an intention to abandon it. *Aldrich v. Olson*, 12 Wn. App. 665, 531 P.2d 825 (1975).
6. For a general discussion of subleasing see Stoebuck, *The Law between Landlord and Tenant in Washington: Part II*, 49 WASH. L. REV. 1013, 1057 (1974).

Chapter 9

1. RCW 59.18.140.
2. The model upon which Washington's Landlord-Tenant Act is based, the Uniform Residential Landlord Tenant Act, restricts the amount of deposits to no more than one month's rent. URLTA §2.101 (a).
3. RCW 59.18.260.
4. RCW 59.18.260.
5. The only reported decisions on damage deposits in this state involve commercial tenants. See *Barrett v. Monro*, 69 Wash. 229, 124 P. 369 (1912); *Smith v. Lambert Transfer Co.*, 109 Wash. 529, 187 P. 362 (1920). It is hard to apply commercial landlord-tenant cases to the residential landlord-tenant context. What may be a fair agreement between two businessmen could be very unfair to insert in a residential form lease or rental agreement.
6. *Williams v. Walker-Thomas Furniture Co.*, 350 F.2d 445 (D.C.Cir. 1965). *Schroeder v. Fageol Motors*, 86 Wn.2d 256, 544 P.2d 20 (1975).
7. This type of clause is called a forfeiture or liquidated damages clause. For a general discussion of forfeitures see Stoebuck, *The Law between Landlord and Tenant in Washington: Part II*, 49 WASH. L. REV. 1013, 1032 (1974); Annot., 106 A.L.R. 292 (1937); Annot., 23 A.L.R.2d 1318 (1952).
8. *Management, Inc. v. Schassberger*, 39 Wn.2d 321, 235 P.2d 293 (1951); *Brower Co. v. Garrison*, 2 Wn. App. 424, 468 P.2d 469 (1970).
9. RCW 59.18.270 explains what the landlord is required to do with deposits during the tenancy.
10. RCW 59.18.280 explains when and how the landlord is to return a refundable deposit.
11. RCW 59.18.280.
12. For a general discussion on the abuses of deposits see Blumberg, *Beyond URLTA: A Program for Achieving Real Tenant Goals*, 11 HARV. C.R.-C.L. L. REV. 1, 18 (1976); Note, *The Residential Lease: Some Innovations for Improving the Landlord-Tenant Relationship*, 3 U.C. D. L. REV. 31, 38–43 (1971).
13. RCW 59.18.280.

Chapter 10

1. For a general history of unlawful detainer actions see TAYLOR, ON LANDLORD AND TENANT §786–794 (7th ed., 1879).
2. RCW 59.18.380.
3. RCW 59.12.010 *et seq*; RCW 59.18.370–.410; the procedure must be strictly followed. *Little v. Catania*, 48 Wn.2d 890, 297 P.2d 255 (1956); *Kessler v.*

Nielsen, 3 Wn. App. 120, 472 P.2d 616 (1970); *Big Bend Land Co. v. Huston*, 98 Wash. 640, 168 P.470 (1917).

4. *Tuschoff v. Westover*, 65 Wn.2d 69, 395 P.2d 630 (1964).

5. RCW 59.12.030. See also *Sowers v. Lewis*, 49 Wn.2d 891, 307 P.2d 1064 (1957) and *Woodward v. Blanchett*, 36 Wn.2d 27, 216 P.2d 228 (1950); Peck, *Landlord And Tenant Notices*, 31 WASH. L. REV. 51 (1956).

6. RCW 59.12.040.

7. *Ferguson v. Hoshi*, 25 Wash. 664, 66 P. 105 (1901).

8. See *Wilson v. Daniels*, 31 Wn.2d 633, 198 P.2d 496 (1948); *Signal Oil Co. v. Stebick*, 40 Wn.2d 599, 245 P.2d 217 (1952).

9. For a general discussion of what constitutes a nuisance see PROSSER, LAW OF TORTS, 592 (3d ed., 1964); Stoebuck, *The Law between Landlord and Tenant in Washington: Part I*, 49 WASH. L. REV. 291, 335–36 (1974).

10. RCW 59.04.050; RCW 59.12.030 (6).

11. RCW 59.18.200; RCW 59.12.030.

12. RCW 4.28.010 *et seq.*

13. RCW 59.12.070 and RCW 59.12.080.

14. An unlawful detainer summons that gives the tenant more than twelve days to respond is effective, however. *Hill v. Hill*, 3 Wn. App. 783, 477 P.2d 931 (1970).

15. *Big Bend Land Co. v. Huston*, 98 Wash. 640, 168 P. 470 (1917); *MacRae v. Way*, 64 Wn.2d 544, 392 P.2d 827 (1964); *Kelly v. Schorzman*, 3 Wn. App. 908, 478 P.2d 769 (1970).

16. *Hill v. Hill*, 3 Wn. App. 783, 477 P.2d 931 (1970).

17. RCW 59.18.370.

18. RCW 59.18.390.

19. RCW 59.18.380.

20. RCW 59.18.380.

21. RCW 59.18.390.

22. *O'Connor v. Matzdorff*, 76 Wn.2d 589, 458 P.2d 154 (1969).

23. RCW 59.18.410 specifies the very limited types of damages the judge or jury may assess against a tenant in an unlawful detainer action. There is no authority for the court to enter a judgment against a tenant for damage done to the dwelling. See *Pine Corp. v. Richardson*, 12 Wn. App. 459, 530 P.2d 696 (1975).

24. RCW 59.18.410; RCW 59.12.190.

25. RCW 59.18.290.

26. RCW 59.18.390.

27. *Kessler v. Nielsen*, 3 Wn. App. 120, 472 P.2d 616 (1970).

28. *Provident Mutual Life Ins. Co. v. Thrower*, 155 Wash. 613, 285 P. 654 (1930).

29. See RCW 59.12.060 and *Kelly v. Schorzman*, 3 Wn. App. 908, 478 P.2d 769 (1970).

30. The defense of breach of the implied warranty of habitability is not in the Landlord-Tenant Act but was created by the court in *Foisy v. Wyman*, 83 Wn.2d 22, 515 P.2d 160 (1973).

31. See *Abstract Investment Co. v. Hutchinson*, 22 Cal. Rptr. 309 (1962).

32. RCW 59.18.240; RCW 59.18.250; See *Edwards v. Habib*, 397 F.2d 687 (D.C. Cir. 1968); *Dickhut v. Norton*, 45 W.2d 309, 173 N.W.2d 297 (1970); *Robinson v. Diamond Housing Corp.*, 463 F.2d 853 (D. C. Cir. 1972).

33. *Hosey v. Club Van Cortlandt*, 299 F. Supp. 501 (S.D. N.Y. 1969) [unlawful for landlord to evict tenant because tenant is exercising constitutionally protected right to protest conditions of building by organizing other tenants]; *Lavoie v. Bigwood*, 457 F.2d 7 (1st Cir. 1972) [unlawful for landlord to evict tenant for complaining to public officials about the management of the premises]; *S. P. Growers Ass'n*

v. Rodriguez, 131 Cal. Rptr. 761 (1976) [unlawful to evict tenants for filing complaints under the Farm Labor Contractor Registration Act, 7 U.S.C. 2041].
34. RCW 59.18.400; set-off is defined in RCW 4.32.110.

Chapter 11

1. RCW 59.18.290. Prior to enactment of the Landlord-Tenant Act, lockouts were prohibited by case law, *Shaffer v. Walther*, 38 Wn.2d 786, 232 P.2d 94 (1951). Today, lockouts and landlord self-help evictions are contrary to statutory and common law. See also Stoebuck, *The Law between Landlord and Tenant in Washington: Part I*, 49 WASH. L. REV. 291, 347 (1974).
2. *Aldrich v. Olson*, 12 Wn. App. 665, 531 P.2d 825 (1975); RCW 59.18.290.
3. RCW 59.18.290.
4. RCW 59.18.310.
5. RCW 59.18.230 (4). If you are not covered by the Landlord-Tenant Act, such a clause might be valid if it meets the requirements for a security interest under RCW 62A.9-101 *et seq*.
6. RCW 59.18.230 (4). See also *Kimball v. Betts*, 99 Wash. 348, 169 P. 849 (1918).
7. RCW 59.18.230 (4).
8. RCW 59.18.300.
9. It is arguable that even the utility cannot terminate service in this case. *Koger v. Guarino*, 412 F. Supp. 1375 (E.D. Pa. 1976).
10. RCW 59.18.300.
11. See generally Stoebuck, *The Law between Landlord and Tenant in Washington: Part I*, 49 WASH. L. REV. 291, note 1 at 347.
12. *Stevens & Co. v. Pratt*, 119 Wash. 232, 205 P. 10 (1922).
13. *Cline v. Altose*, 158 Wash. 119, 290 P. 809 (1930).
14. *Buerkli v. Alderwood Farms*, 168 Wash. 330, 11 P.2d 958 (1932).
15. *King v. King*, 83 Wash. 615, 145 P. 971 (1915).
16. See Attorney General Opinion AGO 1974, No. 10.
17. Seattle Ordinance 106319, Chapter 4, Section 4.17. (April 24, 1977). The Seattle chief of police has the responsibility of enforcing the criminal sections of the Seattle Housing Code. Seattle Ordinance 106319, Chapter 2, Section 2.01. (April 24, 1977).
18. RCW 19.86.010 *et seq*.
19. RCW 19.86.090.

Chapter 12

1. RCW 49.60.222 and RCW 49.60.030 prohibit discrimination in the renting or leasing of property because of race, creed, color, national origin, sex, *or the presence of any sensory, mental, or physical handicap*. In addition, Title VIII of the Civil Rights Act of 1968 (42 U.S.C. §3612 (c)) prohibits discrimination on the basis of race, color, religion, or national origin in the rental of housing; Executive Order 11063 forbids discrimination because of race, color, creed, or national origin in any federally insured or assisted housing; The Civil Rights Act of 1866 (42 U.S.C. §1982) bans *all* discrimination in the rental of property. *Jones v. Alfred H. Mayer Co.*, 392 U.S. 409 (1968). Discrimination in housing is also prohibited by municipal ordinance in many cities. In Spokane, Ordinance No. C-19682 makes discrimination because of race, color, religion, ancestry, or national origin unlawful. Seattle Ordinance No. 104839 prohibits discrimination because of race, color, religion, ancestry, national origin, sex, marital status, sexual orientation, or political ideology.

2. Under both 42 U.S.C. §1982 and 42 U.S.C. §3612 (c) suit can be brought for immediate possession, damages, and attorney's fees. See *Sullivan v. Little Hunting Park, Inc.*, 396 U.S. 229 (1969); *Newman v. Piggy Park Enterprises, Inc.*, 390 U.S. 400 (1968). Suit may also be brought under RCW 49.60.030, which allows the court to stop further violations, award money damages, court costs, and attorney's fees.

3. RCW 59.18.380. See *Abstract Investment Co. v. Hutchinson*, 22 Cal. Rptr. 309 (1962).

4. Send your complaints to:

Fair Housing, Region X
Department of Housing and
Urban Development
1321 Second Avenue
Seattle, Washington 98101

Complaints may be by letter or on a HUD complaint form, which can be obtained from a HUD office or the Post Office. It should be notarized and sent to HUD *within 180 days of the discriminatory act.*

5. The Washington State Human Rights Commission maintains offices in Bellingham, Olympia, Pasco, Seattle, Spokane, Tacoma, and Yakima. The complaint must be filed within six months of the alleged discrimination; RCW 49.60.230.

Chapter 13

1. RCW 12.40.010. Some small claims courts may have a limit of $200.

2. RCW 3.20.060. Call your local district court to get information about its geographic boundaries.

3. RCW 4.28.070; Civil Rules of Justice Court, JCR 4 (e).

4. JCR 4 (h).

5. RCW 4.28.080 (9); JCR 4 (e).

6. Collection procedures include garnishment of wages or bank accounts, RCW 7.33.010 *et seq*; or execution on personal property, RCW 6.04.010 *et seq.*

7. A judgment may be asserted as a set-off or affirmative defense against present or future claims of a landlord. RCW 59.18.110; RCW 59.18.390.

Glossary

Affidavit of Service. A written statement signed in front of a notary public which indicates when, where, and how a defendant was served with legal papers. The statement must be signed by the person who served the papers.

Answer. A legal paper in which the defendant in a lawsuit admits, denies, or claims to lack knowledge about the statements made in the plaintiff's complaint.

Arbitration. A procedure where disputes are resolved by a private, unofficial person selected by the parties.

Complaint. A legal paper in which the plaintiff in a lawsuit states what he is demanding from the defendant and the facts on which he is relying to support his demand.

Constructive Eviction. Actions by a landlord which make a residence so unfit or unpleasant that a tenant is forced to move out.

Default Judgment. A final decision rendered in a lawsuit where the defendant does not show up and present a defense.

Defendant. The person against whom a lawsuit is brought.

District Court. A state court which has the power to hear and decide lawsuits involving less than $1,000.

Exculpatory Clause. A written provision in a lease or rental agreement which excuses a landlord from liability for his own wrongful or negligent actions.

Judgment. The final written decision of a judge which resolves the claims of the parties to a lawsuit and which determines the amount of money the parties owe one another.

Jury. A certain number of persons (either six or twelve) selected to decide factual disputes in a lawsuit.

Lease. An agreement which creates a landlord and tenant relationship, usually for a fixed period of time.

Lessee. The person to whom a residence is leased.

Lessor. The person who leases a residence to a tenant.

Month-to-Month Tenancy. A landlord and tenant relationship in which rent is payable monthly and which continues indefinitely until terminated by one of the parties.

Notary Public. A person authorized to administer oaths and sign and officially seal certain documents.

Order to Show Cause. A legal paper, signed by a judge or court commissioner, which directs a tenant to appear in court at a certain time for a pre-trial hearing on why the landlord should not immediately get what he is asking for in his complaint.

Plaintiff. The person who brings a lawsuit.

Rental Agreement. Any agreement, oral or written, regarding the rules, regulations, terms, and conditions which apply to a tenancy.

Set-off. A money claim which a tenant has against a landlord and which is contained in the tenant's answer to the landlord's complaint. The money claim must have some connection with the landlord-tenant relationship.

Statute. A law adopted by the state legislature.

Summons. A legal document, usually served with a complaint, which directs a defendant to appear and defend a lawsuit within a specific period of time.

Superior Court. A state court which has the power to hear and decide all lawsuits, regardless of the amount of money involved and which has the exclusive power to decide unlawful detainer actions.

Unlawful Detainer Act. A statute which specifies the procedure that a landlord must follow to evict a tenant.

Warranty of Habitability. A promise which the law requires of landlords that a residence will be fit for human habitation.

Washington Supreme Court. The highest court in the state which has the power to hear and decide appeals from lower court decisions.

Writ of Restitution. A legal paper which directs the sheriff to remove a tenant from rental property within a certain amount of time.

Index

Abandonment by tenant: as reason for landlord's entry, 41; of personal property, 47, 49, 78

Answer: to unlawful detainer complaint, 65–66

Appeals: from small claims court judgment, 88

Appliances: landlord's duty to maintain, 15, 16–17; landlord not required to provide, 16–17; tenant required to use properly, 18

Arbitration: selection of arbitrator, 13; of tenant's failure to perform obligations, 18; of repair disputes, 33–34

Attorney General: assistance for tenants, 81

Attorneys: tenants' need for, 3, 68, 72; selecting, 3–4

Attorney's fees: amount of, 6; when awarded, 6, 13, 14, 36, 40, 47, 55, 66, 69, 71, 76, 78, 79, 81, 82

Bids: for repairs, 30

Boarding house residents: not covered by Landlord-Tenant Act, 5

Bonds: required of landlord in unlawful detainer actions, 68; to prevent pretrial eviction, 68; to prevent post-trial eviction, 71

Building codes: landlord's failure to repair as violation of, 34

Building department: records of building and housing code violations, 8; complaints to, 34

Businesses: not covered by Landlord-Tenant Act, 6

Children: landlord's exclusion of permissible, 22

Cleaning fee, 50

Common areas: landlord to maintain, 15

Complaint. See Summons and complaint

Constructive eviction: defined, 79–80; as result of utility shutoff, 79; because of repair problems, 36

Counterclaims: by landlord, 57–58, 85, 87

Damage: landlord's liability for, 13, 38, 40; tenant's liability for, 18, 49; by sublessee, 49; deposits, 50

Default judgment: in unlawful detainer actions, 65–66; in small claims court, 87

Deposits: generally, 50–58; interest on, 53; recovery of, 53, 54–57

Discrimination: as defense to unlawful detainer action, 73; defined, 82; remedies for, 82–83

Electricity: landlord's duty to provide, 15, 28; tenant's duty to use properly, 18

Entry by landlord: when prohibited, 14, 41, 43

Eviction: before trial, 6; for tenant's failure to care for dwelling, 19; for nonpayment of rent, 20; stopped by posting bond, 68, 71; sheriff's procedure, 71

Eviction notices: when required, 60;